The Woodstock Bridge

The Woodstock Bridge

A Journey To Discover Your Spirit

By
Gregory Drambour

SB Published by Sacred Bear Press

www.SacredBear.com
Inquiries: Publisher@SacredBear.com
Orders: Orders@SacredBear.com

Library of Congress Control Number: 2002104351

Publisher's Cataloging-in-Publication

Drambour, Gregory.
The Woodstock Bridge : a journey with two warriors / by Gregory Drambour. – 1st ed.
p. cm.
LCCN 2002104351
ISBN 0-9719825-1-1

1. Self-actualization (Psychology) 2. Spiritual life. 3. Indians of North American—Religion. I. Title.

BF637.S4D73 2002 158.1
QBI02-701450

FIRST EDITION

10 9 8 7 6 5 4 3 2 1

Book Design: Calvin Ki [www.ntcomudesign.com]
Cover Art: *Between Eagle & Hawk* by Dona Mares. © Dona Mares
Author Portrait: Photographed by Jane Marcy. © Jane Marcy
Printed in Canada on acid-free paper.

See back page for information on purchasing a fine art print of the orginal painting on the cover.

For more information about the author, recommended reading, and other resources, go to: www.WoodstockBridge.com

Acknowledgments

It was the spirit of the Native American Indian that led me to write this book. My relationship with E.C., Black Hawk and Spotted Eagle reflects itself throughout. Credit is due, not to us but to the spirit that speaks through the book. I thank that spirit humbly for the honor.

I thank E.C., Black Hawk and Spotted Eagle for their time and openness. I consider the lives they lead part of the investment needed for this book. Never would I have imagined its existence, but others obviously had, among them David Dowd, who I thank for the suggestion and brilliant support! I am beginning to see how ones life can lead to places unknown.

The angels who have helped me throughout my life influenced much of what is written here. It is with pride and pleasure that I take this opportunity to honor them: Carol Drambour, Michael Bailey, Winnie S., David B., Ron M., Kris Heath, David and Marisa Lerner, Red Garrison, Michael Cindrich, Janis Conti, Dicken Bettenger, Donnie Yance, Lou Cohen, Christine Vlachos, Calvin Ki,

Dori Warren, and Drs. Berson and Camacho.

I would like to thank Richard Carlson, Joseph Bailey, Gordon Bird, and George Horse Capture, Jr. for the wonderful quotes. Their endorsements mean a great deal to me.

My thanks to Syd Banks, Carlos Castaneda, Richard Bach, and Dan Millman for their powerful teachings. They have had a profound influence on my life .

To my brother R.B., "Thank you for keeping me safe. Your loyalty will not be forgotten."

During the writing, my friend Mary Brancatto spoke the words that kept me on the path. I say to her, "Ho."

I send my laughter and thanks to George Allen Cooper, alias Dad, an original member of the "Beat" generation, for the education and the many humorous adventures.

My heart stands with those departed ancestors. I hope I have brought them honor: Marie, Popsy, Rudolph, Friedrich, William, and my brother, Robert, who left me his determination.

Most especially to M., I say, "Thank you for keeping me well during those past years and your loyalty; it is unequaled. I have not forgotten nor will I ever."

My attorney, Egon Dumler, my agent, Richard Barber, and my mentor, Seymour Lisker are all symbols to me of a world gone by. It is with their loyalty and support that I have been able to weather those moments of feeling alone in the sea of "the business." I thank them and offer them my grateful allegiance.

To Eileen, who lived part of the adventure with me,

I say, "Thank you for your love and unconditional support in that time. I am honored to have known you."

My deepest gratitude to Dona Mares for her commitment and devotion to creating the painting, "Between Eagle & Hawk". She has honored us. She is my sister in spirit.

To my other friends and relatives along the path I say, "I have not forgotten and hold you close in my heart."

To the children I encountered every so often who changed my day, my world, by smiling at me, I say, "Thank you," and I thank God for putting them in my path.

"Thank you, A.M.B.. Your preciousness, openness, and love inspire me each and every day. You have saved my life too many times to count. I feel so lucky to have you in my life."

To my mother I say, "The writing of the book is the only possible way of thanking you for all you have given me. Without your unconditional support, I would not have been able to write the book in the way it perhaps needed to be written."

All the names spoken here, have written this book with me. I will not retreat from this. They are the warriors I walk beside on the path. If I am but a fleeting refection of them, I am honored. A Ho.

To my mother, a true warrior.
She has my admiration, respect, and loyalty.

Introduction

Dear Reader,

Inside of you lives a warrior's spirit waiting to be recognized. This spirit holds many of the answers you may be searching for. It knows from every act there is something to be learned, that the journey on Earth is not about what you do but *how* you do it. A warrior discovers the answers in the *how*.

Spirit doesn't have to be taught but *noticed*. Have you ever walked down a street and suddenly noticed there was a beautiful sky overhead? Spirit is no different – its right in front of you, just be *open* to noticing it. When you catch sight of it, spirit will lead you to the freedom and happiness you've wished for.

Here's a clue: As you read you may become aware you're following the words to closely, you've begun to analyze and assess – the reading isn't fun. Again, you *just notice* it. For now, let me suggest you don't *do anything about it* – don't try to fix it. Your instinct will know what to do. Just be aware, then let it go! And whatever you do – PLEASE DON'T TRY AND FIGURE OUT WHAT I'M SAYING!

It can seem difficult to notice the bridge to your spirit. I lost sight of it many times as I wrote about my experiences. For example, I would confer with my Sioux friends, Black Hawk and Spotted Eagle, on my accuracy about Native American traditions – it was important to me to be impeccable. After what I guess were too many accuracy-checks, this is what they said: "*What is traditional, is what is in your heart!*"

When I heard those words I felt a window open that I didn't know was closed. I knew that spirit was about seeing and crossing the bridge from one's heart to one's life – and this is what this book is about.

A wise friend once said to me, "What you're looking for is a little secret that nobody can find but you." You can find it with or without this book. Maybe there are some pointers in these pages for you. Maybe my experiences will open a closed window. The old ones say the return of the warriors is now; they have been called back and their spirit sparks something in us. Adventures are waiting right inside you and *you* have the passion to take them on. Let *how* you read my book be an adventure. Let it be the place you start to notice the bridge to your heart.

So, begin here, on the first page. If you feel good right now, that's what you're looking for. Read my book from that place of well-being and I promise the world will crack open and secrets and insights will rush out! If you notice you feel bad, put the book down. Read it the next day, week, or year. God has His own schedule. Or as Black Hawk and Spotted Eagle call Him, "Tunkshila," which translates to mean Grandfather. Since my experiences, I find myself whispering, "Grandfather, thank you."

Meet my friends, Black Hawk and Spotted Eagle...

Chapter One

Perhaps the last time I felt right with myself and the world was at the Woodstock Concert in 1969. These feelings began to return when I met Black Hawk Who Walks The Wind, a Sioux Indian. This is the story of that friendship.

I was nineteen at the concert, and at the end of those three days, I felt the power of unity. I felt we had shown the Establishment that we were to be reckoned with. My belief that the individual can make a difference had never been stronger – anything was possible.

Soon after Woodstock I slowly and unthinkingly joined the system I had fought. I found myself working for the dreaded enemy – the corporation. I quickly moved up the ladder and collected all the medals: government issue BMW, a share in a co-op, membership in several prestigious clubs, and a divorce.

Then vestiges of betrayed ideals began to appear. I ignored them at first, until the seventh crossing of paths with an old comrade-in-arms from the "Movement." In an animated conversation with him on the pluses and minuses of the new BMW, my speech about "cornering" blasted through the sealed sixties-compartment of my memory. I quickly excused myself, feigning an appointment with my therapist – or was it stockbroker? The actual finish has always been a blur.

At that point I counted years. Too many years since the concert. Too many years since I had shouted, "No more war." I crawled into a deep hole within the confines of my co-op. The tenth day of hibernation brought a message from God: sell everything and return to Woodstock. I knew how to follow orders. So I quit my job, sold my apartment and all belongings owned by me and my pal the bank, and set off for Woodstock where I was sure answers to my questions about life lay waiting.

I had a lot of questions. When was the last time I had really laughed? When had I really enjoyed something the way I used to? Why couldn't I find a woman? Why was I so anxious for space travel? Why had I given in, and why so easily? My departure was surprisingly unheralded. Neither the corporation, my fellow share-holders in the co-op, my BMW mechanic, nor anyone else in authority seemed to care.

I reached Woodstock quickly. One small house and a few friends later, I discovered that whichever God had spoken had lied. There were no answers in Woodstock, only a bunch of artists and tourists hanging about. I soon tired of reminiscing with other dropouts in local bars. I retreated into limbo. I no longer cared about answers and dreams, nor did I make any effort to find them. I had enough part-time work, fleeting female companionship, and bitterness to survive. Why try then fail, as I once had done? One person couldn't make a difference. Who ever gave birth to the silly notion that one could, anyway? What the hell was there to fight for? What could you stand against, now? Where was the possibility of a change, of having an effect? The issues were too big, and the bureaucracy and powers-that-be too powerful, too insulated.

The day of change came in the fall. I went to the town green where musicians and sixties-type people congregated on afternoons to jam and talk. I sat by myself as I had since my return to Woodstock. I peered around as I always do. Then a chill went through me. A couple of seconds later a brief gust of warm wind blew over me. I felt as if the wind had spoken to me. For a moment I felt at peace. Then the feeling left me as quickly as it had come, and I felt even more alone.

I tried to retreat into numbness, but I sensed somebody staring at me. I looked around, but there was no one with his eyes on me and no one looking as if he had quickly turned away. Then I noticed a large, black bird perched in an oak tree across the street, staring at me. The bird was quite dignified and held his head high. We stared at each other a good bit of time. For some reason I did not think it unusual for this bird to be staring at me, or me at him. I sensed we were connecting, reaching an understanding of some sort. I felt slightly more alive than I had for some time.

I turned away for an instant, then back. He was gone. Then I sensed someone standing beside me, although I had not heard or seen anyone approach. I looked up and saw a man who looked to be in his late thirties. He was simply dressed in tan, loose-fitting pants and shirt. He had long black hair and a dark, reddish complexion. His features were sharp, fierce. But the fierceness neither frightened nor intimidated me. I felt protected by it. He stood absolutely still and centered. He seemed rooted in the ground. But what I first noticed was his presence, his dignity, the deep humility he emanated. Humility was the one characteristic in another person that could still effect me, still penetrate my defenses.

He held his head high, and his black eyes spoke to me as if he knew me. Their intensity unnerved me, and I looked away quickly. But from the corner of my eye, I saw that neither his gaze nor his posture had altered. I kept my eyes averted; he raised his left arm slowly and proudly toward me, with the palm facing me and fingers spread wide. He held his arm there for a moment, then pressed his hand flat against his chest. He knew I was watching, and he kept his hand on his chest, waiting for a response. I rose, as if in a trance, and faced him. I raised my hand in a similar gesture and then brought my hand to my chest. The motivation to do this came from a place inside that was foreign to me, but a place I then felt I knew better than any other.

He smiled a warm smile. I, who hadn't permitted myself a smile in years, smiled back. For a moment the world outside us seemed not to exist. After a time I reached across the space separating us and offered my hand in greeting.

"I'm John," I said. He didn't shake my hand but firmly

grasped my forearm.

"I am called Black Hawk," he said.

His voice was deep, and he spoke slowly, as if behind each word rested a separate world. As we stood joined – even though the distance between us had not altered – his eyes seemed to move closer to mine. I sensed he was trying to understand me. It felt comforting.

"John, it is good to see you," he said, pressing two fingers of his left hand together and raising them to his eyes, then pushing the fingers toward me. I found it beautiful, the way he spoke and gestured in the same moment. It made me feel he was right there with me, that his words were sincere.

"It's nice to meet you, too," I offered. "Is this your first visit to Woodstock?"

"Yes."

"Where are you from?"

"West from Woodstock," he responded. His smile now seemed mischievous.

"West from Woodstock." What the hell does that mean, I thought, but something stopped me from asking.

"John, what celebration is this?" he asked, sweeping his hand around to include the musicians and the hundred or so people who filled the sidewalks and the green.

"No celebration," I said. "Just a bunch of tourists who we always get on the weekends and musicians who don't have anywhere else to play. It's always like this."

"Yes?" he said. His face lit up. "The music has much spirit."

"It's okay," I responded.

"Does it not feel good to you?" he asked.

Now his smile annoyed me. Who is this guy? I thought. Isn't it a little soon to be confronting me, getting personal?

"It's not a matter of it not feeling good, I don't pay a lot of attention to them," I responded.

"Do you ever join them?"

What an inane question. "No. I don't play an instrument." I waited for another attack, but he remained silent, looking at me with what seemed to be compassion. For what? I wondered.

He continued to look around. Emotions played across his face at each new scene he took in. I followed his eyes to two little girls of seven or so, playing in front of the crystal shop. They were laughing, chasing each other in a game of tag. He let out a wonderful laugh at their antics, and I was sure he was going to run across the street and join in. Hell, his enjoyment made me want to run over and join the game.

"We have a game much like that where I come from," he said.

Now we were getting somewhere. "And that's west of here?" I asked with my own mischievous smile.

"Yes, west." He laughed. "It is a place I think you have been many seasons ago."

"Could you give me a hint? Where west?"

"You call it Da-ko-ta."

"South Dakota?"

"Yes, South Dakota."

"No, I've never been there."

There was that annoying smile again, as if he knew something I didn't. This was starting to get weird. Any initial connection I had felt to this guy was gone.

I considered saying "nice meeting you, pal" and leaving, or holding my ground and waiting for him to leave.

"Have you lived in this place long?" he said.

"Too long."

"Is it a strong place to live?"

"What do you mean 'strong'?" I wasn't letting him run these weird questions by me unchecked any longer.

"Does it provide you with what you need?"

"I'm not sure I know what you mean," I countered.

"Where I live, the earth offers me shelter, clothing, food. The land makes my heart full." As his hands wove the picture, I saw the place he spoke of, and my heart leapt at the possibility that such a place existed.

"Oh, you live off the land? I've always wanted to do that. How long have you been living that way?"

"From the beginning," he said.

A chill went through me.

Chapter Two

The chill left me inexplicably sad. Perhaps it was the sound of his voice, which seemed to move into my body. It was like a low hum.

"You mean you've always lived like that?" I asked.

"Yes, I am of the Sioux nation."

I didn't want to question him on his Indian heritage, behaving no better than the tourists who feasted on Woodstock.

"Are you visiting friends up here?"

With that smile and that same gesture of moving two fingers slowly from his eyes toward me, he responded, "I have come to see you, John."

"What?" I blurted. "What do you mean, you've come to see me?"

"Does this anger you?" The kindness with which he asked defused my anger. As I took a breath to get my bearings, he watched me with concern.

"No, I'm not angry," I said. "You're just scaring the hell out of me. I mean, what the hell is going on here? Did somebody send you from New York? That's it, isn't it? Was it my parents?"

"No one sent me," he said gently. "I have come in the hope that I can offer you…" His open hands gestured, himself, help. Only my worn bitterness held back the tears.

I was disorientated. I sat down. He did the same. I remained quiet for a time and watched weekend - Woodstock. People up from the city walked by. They seemed alien to me. With each passing year, my contempt for them had grown deeper. I spared only the children and the old people my judgments.

Black Hawk continued to watch me as he had done since we first met. I felt no resentment at his watching; it comforted me.

"How do you know me?" I asked.

"The story is good. For it is given to us from Tunkashila [pronounced, Ta-kon-sh-la]. But the words will not find your heart, only your mind."

"What does that mean?"

"Your mind will hear, not your spirit."

I knew what he meant; the sixties had taught me that much. But I wasn't about to admit it. My head was so caught in its own defenses that I might hear nothing of his story. Still I stayed quiet, conjuring a strategy to extract the story from him. He saw through the plot and laughed.

"Have patience, John. Open your heart to the spirit inside. The winged, the hawk called to you. The hawk's spirit is strong. It will guide you."

"How do you know about the bird?"

He laughed again. What was with all this laughing?

"What's so funny?"

"Your mind." He said.

"Thanks! You drop in from nowhere – excuse me, west a place called Da-ko-ta, you say you know me, and have come to visit!"

"Yes!"

"Yes?! Okay, let's skip how you know me. I'll just go along with being deranged for a bit. Why exactly are you here?"

"You do not stand alone on your journey. Have you sought to know of this, here in your place? Has this kept you warm in the winter of your thoughts?"

My place? Come to think of it, over the years I had seen very few people sit there. Perhaps they felt the negative vibe.

"Which journey are we speaking of?" I asked.

"The journey of your spirit," he said, with such serious concern that I felt the fool for being obnoxious.

"I'm not sure I know what you mean," I said by way of an apology.

"The spirit is the God within you, Tunkashila." He looked to the sky.

"Tunkashila?"

"God. Everything here is of Tunkashila." He motioned to include the trees, the sky, the earth. "Your spirit is what belongs to your Father and my Father, not your mind."

I had never taken much of a stand on God. I believed in Him, but what exactly I believed was undefined. So I was curious to hear Black Hawk's interpretation. And spirit? I was unsure of his meaning. I imagined it was synonymous with wisdom, instinct, and another hundred labels. Hell, wasn't this the question we had wrestled with from the sixties till now? What is it inside us that speaks with wisdom and without conflict? How do we find that voice? How do we keep it?

"No. I guess if I think about it, I'm not alone in my journey," I said.

"It is good," he said with a pleased smile. "I feared you would close your eyes to others. We are all of the same Father and Mother; our journeys are different but also the same."

"But what is spirit?"

"Spirit is the path without words."

I knew that. What good did it do me?

"John, come." He beckoned and I followed him across the street to the opposite sidewalk.

We strolled along, past the shops. He had said journeys were the same but different. Had I really understood what he was getting at with "did I think I was not alone"? Why did he think I had ignored it?

"What did you mean by…"

He held up his hand to stop me, smiling that damn smile again.

"What? Can't I ask a question?"

"Let us walk and feel the power of this place. Like Tunkashila, the spirit of this place wishes to be honored. Then it will speak to you. For this place is part of you, as you are part of it."

He spoke confidently and left no room for argument, so I kept my mouth shut as I walked beside him, trying to find that place of spirit. It seemed to be on the other side of a door that only opened one way. And because I was on the wrong side, I felt cheated. More than cheated, because I knew what lay behind it: Peace.

He stopped when he saw a couple in their late seventies sitting on a bench across the street. I had seen them around town; their closeness had always touched me. As he watched the couple, his head rose higher, his bearing became even more fierce, and his eyes grew darker. It was the stance of a warrior in the presence of those he must protect and honor. Emotion surged in me, and I gathered strength to steel myself against it. I gave up the effort when the old man, seeing Black Hawk, stood and faced him with great dignity. Time stood still as the two warriors crossed a bridge of respect. I had an urge to run away, for the emotions of this silent world were beyond my control.

Black Hawk bid a silent farewell to the old man. I remained by his side as he continued down the street. He delighted at each shop window and each person we passed, and this turned my fear to contempt. Didn't he see the shallowness of these tourists and the traps set for them?

We circled back toward the green. "There is much power here, John." He took a moment then said flatly, "It is a good place to live."

"I don't agree with you. All that's here is a tourist site."

"You live here," he said.

"Yeah, so?"

"If this place does not give you what you need, why remain?"

"That's a long story."

He watched my eyes closely, taking in my words as if I had said something of great importance. I felt unnerved and looked away. We approached the green, and he veered toward a young man in his twenties who was playing a guitar and singing softly. We stopped a few feet from him and listened as he sang of lost love. Black Hawk listened intently, squatting on his haunches. He and the singer exchanged a comfortable smile which annoyed me. Then Black Hawk sang. The language was foreign, but his words joined as if in a marriage to the song of the young man. Black Hawk's voice was low and quiet and threaded with strength. It resonated with a feeling that bridged language. It reached deep inside me and opened the door to my heart. Black Hawk motioned me to join in. I retreated like a scared animal to a safe distance where no one could force me to sing.

A pretty teenage girl holding a wooden flute approached and silently asked permission to join in. They welcomed her. Her playing was haunting. Black Hawk and the young man stopped and listened as I did, mesmerized by the sound. Black Hawk's eyes closed briefly. The trust and wholeness of his listening angered me. The girl stopped and beckoned to Black Hawk. Her eyes revealed a pain far too great for such a young girl to have known. Black Hawk opened his eyes and looked directly at her. With his next breath, he began an Indian chant in a rhythmic wave of sound which I somehow knew came from the place of no words, the place of spirit. The music and chanting took me back to the sadness I had felt when Black Hawk spoke of "the beginning." What was it about, I wondered?

They finished and exchanged smiles of gratitude. I felt a fool and regretted my timidity in not joining. We began to walk away and I wanted to continue my interrogation, including what had transpired between him and the old man and then the girl. But I sensed that all I would get would be his wave to halt my questions.

"Tell me, John, can you walk from Woodstock to the trees?" he asked.

"You mean the woods?" He nodded. "Sure, it's a bit of walk, though, to really get away from everything."

"Will you walk with me?" he asked formally.

I looked down at the ground, up at the sky, anywhere to avoid his eyes. I sensed that with each of his acts he was showing me the path without words. To travel on it seemed impossible. It was beyond my strength. Feeling defeated and resigned, I raised my eyes and as I had first seen him, he stood with dignity. It touched me and brought a spark of hope. Suddenly, without another thought, for the first time in years, I raised my head a bit.

Chapter Three

We walked in silence for a couple of miles on the side of a paved road through a thick, uninhabited forest. I wondered where we were going and began to question the wisdom of walking off into a remote area with a stranger. I pondered how I could excuse myself politely and head back to Woodstock. Then, over the other forest sounds, I heard a bird give a distinct whistle. Black Hawk stopped abruptly, scanned the area, and then moved into the trees. I followed. His new course was so focused that I gathered we were close to wherever we were going. I postponed the idea of retreat. We walked through dense growth – no trail. I didn't want to appear to be weak-hearted, so I kept quiet. Compared with his sure-footedness, my blundering through the brush was embarrassing. I tried to strike up a conversation to find some secure way of redeeming myself.

"Where are we headed?" I asked.

"The spirit calls to us, John. We must have faith that it will guide us."

He looked toward the treetops to indicate the bird

"whistle."

"You mean that bird back at the road?" I asked. He nodded. Ridiculous. It was a only a bird calling. How did he know…? He interrupted my thoughts.

"If a man, a friend, calls to you and says, 'John, come, the path is here,' would you follow?"

"It depends." He waited for me to elaborate. "I mean, I don't understand what that has to do with the bird."

"The bird, the winged, like the four-legged, the animal, and the two-legged, man, are all of Tunkashila. It is Tunkashila, God, that gives us all spirit. The mind, fear, tells us that we are not the same, that we are better than the four-legged and the winged. But who is it that lives from the land with no shelter, no protection? Who is it that has lived before the two-legged walked the earth? Who is it that gives of itself so that we may feed ourselves? They live from the place of spirit and Tunkashila provides for them. When my brother the winged calls to me, I listen to his words with gentleness in my heart. I know that his spirit is strong and true, and not of mind.

"Most of what he said was beyond me. Animals living off the land – I would have liked to have challenged him on that. If I had fur to keep me warm and teeth to protect me, I could live off the land, too. But I felt it the better part of wisdom to keep my mouth shut. We trekked on. I kept my eyes open for snakes, the dreaded deer tick, and other carnivores.

"Mother Earth will protect us, John, for we walk softly upon her, with knowing in our heart that it is the earth that gives us life. She is our true Mother. When I pass on, my shell will decay in the earth and go back to soil. It may give life to the tree. That is why we say Grandfather Tree. Plants may spring from that soil. That is why we say Plant People. They are our children, as we are theirs. The grass comes from that soil and feeds the deer, and in this way, the deer becomes our relative. And one day the deer may give of itself to feed and cloth the two-legged. This is why we say, the land is the blood and bones of our ancestors."

That made a certain amount of sense to me. But I feared the thousands of environmental ramifications that sense would bring into focus. What good could anyone do, anyway? Particularly one person? Environmental groups had tried. The effect on the big picture was minimal, if that.

"Well, we're not doing a very good job of taking care of the earth," I said.

"I have seen what you speak of," he said. "The two-legged walk with fear, and their fear steps on the land they walk upon. They walk with the mind. For they know that if they walked with spirit, they could no longer hurt their Mother.

"Death flies above the two-leggeds' thoughts and says to them, they will return to the Mother, to the Earth, when death takes them. So the two-legged seek to destroy that which they fear: the Earth.

"I see the whites put their shells in wooden boxes to keep the earth from taking them into her. But the spirit has already left that body and gone to Tunkashila."

"So you think we don't take care of the environment

because we fear death?" I asked.

"The answer lies within each man and woman."

"You mean that for each person there's a different reason?"

"Do you remember what we have spoken of in Woodstock, that each journey is the same but different?"

"Yes."

"It is so."

"What do you mean?"

"The deer comes to our moccasin path. Does he walk across it? Does he walk inside our tracks? Does he walk on the side?"

"I don't know." He smiled. Great!

"Come on, you're not going to leave me hanging!" I pleaded.

"From where?" he asked.

"What do you mean from where?"

"Hanging from where?" He looked around curiously at the trees.

What is this, Abbott and Costello? A language problem maybe? Was he making fun of me?

"Forget it," I said, stomping ahead of him. I crashed through the woods, breaking branches that lay across my path, and crushing small plants under my feet – all without a second thought. Then I stepped in a small concealed hole, and fell flat on my face. This drew laughter from my new-found friend. I was positive my nose was broken. But after much prodding and continued hilarity from the enemy, I decided to wait for the swelling in silence.

"The Grandfather Trees and Plant People have spoken," he said, smiling.

"Who's spoken?"

He laughed so hard that he had trouble breathing. I tried hard to hold it back but a wonderful laugh burst from my lips. I didn't remember the last time I laughed at myself. It felt good.

"Do you see?" he asked again, with the powerful gesture of two fingers pressed together, then moving from his eyes towards me.

"Yes, I see," I answered, making the same gesture.

"I didn't walk on the earth as if it were part of me and I suffered her response of mutual disrespect."

"It is good." He got up and held out his hand. "There is much to speak about, John, let us walk further on."

I reached for his hand.

Chapter Four

"Do you hear, John?" He stopped our journey through the forest abruptly. We had been going through a clear, walkable section for about two miles.

"No, what?" He stood absolutely still, listening. I focused my hearing. He turned to me and made the gesture away from his eyes. I took it to mean I was doing something wrong.

"What?" I whispered.

"Listen with the spirit."

"Oh, why didn't you say so?!" We grinned at each other and remained still. Then, from nowhere, a beautiful sight walked within twenty feet of us. It was a deer, a buck, with antlers reaching to the sky.

I watched the buck, fearing even to breathe lest he dart away. Black Hawk stood a step in front of me. I could see he had found a long-lost friend.

The deer turned its head and peered at us as if to say we were no threat, just another part of the forest. Those eyes exuded a trust and a serenity which I had never before witnessed. But it was something even more alien. I had neither the vocabulary nor the knowledge to explain it, but I could see it. Do you see? I thought, echoing Black Hawk's question. This puzzled me. Then what I had "seen" was lost.

Black Hawk slowly raised his arm and offered the deer the proud greeting he had first given me: fingers spread wide, palm up. Then he spoke a greeting. I could not understand the words, but the message of respect was evident. "A Ho," he said, pronouncing the first syllable "ah." The deer did not budge his gaze from us. Black Hawk walked on. Why, I thought, couldn't we wait to the last possible minute and watch until the stag had run away? I felt that would sound childish, so I didn't say anything. But I still wondered why.

As we moved through the woods which stretched for miles, I began to get a feel for the way the trees and foliage flowed, of how not to fight them. The forest wrapped itself around me. I was a part of it. I trusted that the path of least resistance would show itself to me. But I went in and out of this feeling: out, when I was conscious of it, and wondered how and where it came from; and in, when I gave myself fully to it.

We stopped for a rest. I related to Black Hawk what I had been thinking, and he told me a story, a version of which I had heard or read before. But then I understood it differently. I "got it."

"When I was Hokshila back home –" he began.

"What's that?" I didn't want to miss anything

"A little boy."

"Oh."

"The elders taught me that, when I played in the great river, I should not fight it. I should let the water carry me where it wished. They taught me that the river will always take you back to the bank. This is the way. Other people meet their death in the water, for they believe they are strong and will return to where they first went into the water. This is mind, John: 'I am strong. I will not let this take me down there, I am coming back. I am more powerful. I am better.' They meet their death. "I go downstream. I am carried by the great river. My spirit is given strength and healed by its spirit. For the water is the blood of Mother Earth.

"The deer is a powerful sign, John. Soon it will be the time of the telling of how I came upon you. The deer has spoken to me that your spirit will hear, will see the gift Tunkashila has given us."

"How do you know he was a sign?" I asked.

The smile again.

"No, come on, I'm serious. I want to know."

"How I can speak of what has no words?"

"Okay, well…I mean…what did you feel?"

"To see what is in front of you on the path, you must open your eyes," he responded. His hands glided through the air stressing "open."

"I have to open my eyes?" I questioned back. "I don't understand. It's a metaphor, right? A symbol?"

"It is so." He beamed.

I mumbled to myself, "To see what's in front of me…

open my eyes."

Laughing, he said, "Come, let us go to the place that will call to us. You cannot find the answer to your question with the mind. You know of this."

"I do?"

"Yes," he answered and picked up the pace, giving me no chance to question him further. And, man, I hate those riddle responses. But I didn't want to fall in any more holes, so I held myself in check.

Thoughts and questions about his statements kept racing through my head as we moved over the terrain. Every attempt to stop them only made the thoughts run faster and the internal dialogue become more detailed. After about twenty minutes, I thought if I asked nicely enough, he might offer advice. My trust was building. I had learned something since I'd met him. I never felt as if he was lecturing me or even teaching me. His manner of communicating was never intrusive. It was as if he were giving me a gift.

I called out to him. He was ten feet ahead. "Black Hawk."

He turned back, smiling at me.

"Forget it." I laughed.

"No, come on, tell me." He imitated my whining perfectly.

"It is so," I countered in my own imitation of him.

We started cracking up and stopped our trek, trying to catch our breath. We stumbled around aimlessly, holding our stomachs. Just as the last laugh ripped through us, Black Hawk said again, "Come on, tell me".

"It is so," I repeated.

We went off again. We must have been quite a sight, there, in the middle of the forest, prancing around, doubled over like two leprechauns, begging with our hands, "No more, no more."

Finally, we calmed down, looked at each other and smiled, his smile a little more devilish than mine.

"No, don't," I pleaded. "Let's go."

We continued, gliding through the beautiful trees. Then I thought, that's funny, my head has quieted down.

Chapter Five

How the hell did I get up here?! We were not walking up a hill but scaling a mountain, mostly of rock. I hadn't noticed until I had turned around and looked down. This was a mistake. Fear ripped through me.

I remember we had started to walk uphill, and it had gradually gotten steeper and steeper. I had simply played follow the leader, thinking nothing of the steepness. I hadn't noticed the first time I had to reach up for a hold on a ledge. I suppose I was in a semitrance from the consistent, rhythmic pace.

I consider myself a fairly sturdy fellow, but my mountaineering experience is limited to the Empire State Building elevators.

I looked down and thought, this is not good. I gazed up at my friend, Black Hawk, the goat, who seemed to be having a fine time. I thought maybe I should turn around before it got worse. But going back downhill didn't appear to be a stroll, either.

Before we reached the mountain, Black Hawk had

slowed every now and then for a close examination of a tree or plant, and had given special attention to rocks; he really enjoyed the rocks. His brief observations were simple, never analytical, and were related with a peaceful, friendly feeling. After a visit with a rock, we would sometimes veer off in a new direction.

After I had looked down, my climbing turned awkward and tentative. Between each ungripping and gripping of a ledge, I had visions of my head smashing into jagged, flesh-ripping boulders. I thought maybe I should inquire as to how long I had to live.

"Are we close?" I asked, my voice deep, like a true mountain man.

"Close?" he asked.

"To the place."

He stopped.

"Rest," he said. He sat down on the steep incline, facing down the mountain. It was a long way down.

"Here?" I asked.

He checked around to see if there was something wrong with the spot.

"Is there a hole?!" he asked

"Very funny. I just thought… Never mind."

It was no easy feat to sit down at that spot. One move in either direction and I was a goner. Black Hawk was perfectly relaxed and enjoying the view. I hadn't noticed the view in the climb; I had been too busy trying to remember how the "Hail Mary" went. (When in doubt revert to Catholicism.) I maneuvered myself into a secure, wedged position, then leaned on my knees a few degrees too far.

"Whoa," I yelled, toppling. Black Hawk grabbed my arm and balanced me.

"Thanks," I offered. "So?"

"So," he retorted.

"Is this a rest stop, or is there a specific reason why we stopped at this goat resort? This isn't the place, is it?!"

"No." He laughed. "What is it that you fear here?"

"Nothing, I'm fine," I answered coolly. My knuckles were turning white from the grip I held.

He waited.

"Okay... Well, I wouldn't really call it fear. I'm just a little uncomfortable."

"Where does it come from?"

"Well, because one wrong step and it's see you later, goodbye."

"Where does it come from?" he persisted.

"I don't know what you mean. It comes from my fear of dying."

"Does fear of death come from spirit?"

I didn't answer. I had a creeping suspicion that I knew where this was leading.

"Does fear come from mind?"

I nodded reluctantly.

"Why do we climb this mountain?" he asked in a serious tone.

"Because we're going to a place to talk of how you know me," I said.

"Are we on a journey?" he asked.

"Yes, I guess you could call it that."

"For you, is this journey to feed the spirit, to learn of the spirit inside you?"

I was too taken back by his words to respond.

"We follow the path, for we have spoken to the Rock People and the Plant People, and they have guided us. If we were taken by Tunkashila and met death, we would face the Great Spirit as warriors, for our death was given on a journey of spirit."

He regarded me with those dark eyes. They were filled with tears and dignity. A great wave of emotion rushed through me, and I was afraid that if I spoke, I'd set it free or that what he spoke of would become a part of me. Perhaps it already was. This new part of me felt like a home I'd been kept from – a place of dignity and honor where I was willing to give my life in pursuit of spiritual strength and knowledge. I sensed a piece of the puzzle almost fall into place. Perhaps pursuit of spirit was synonymous with pursuit of the ideals of freedom and happiness. Ideals I had lost, had forgotten. It was a pursuit that had held no greater value. If you had to die, what better way to meet God?

Black Hawk was right, it was a journey of the spirit – the part of me that cared about myself and the world. As we sat on the rocks our eyes met again, and a silent understanding passed between us. It was difficult for me to open up. He knew and accepted this. I wanted to express my thanks for his friendship, so I rose and took the lead up the mountain.

I reached the top quickly. Strangely, I didn't remember the climb. I felt I'd given something to the mountain, though. Perhaps it was my trust, my respect. We stood gazing out across the brightly colored, autumn valley. I felt good, neither tired nor hungry. Twilight was creeping down. We looked behind us. About a mile off was a small lake.

"For the wisdom that has been shown us, let us make offering to the Grandfather Mountain," said Black Hawk.

"How do we do that?

"He took a small, deer-skin pouch out of his pocket, opened it and gently took out a handful of tobacco.

"The heart of our Mother rests under us. We see with our heart, with our spirit, a place to make small opening. We return to the earth with our prayers that which is sacred, the tobacco. In this way, we give back."

"What does the tobacco represent?" I asked.

"The tobacco is sacred to my people. It was given to us in the beginning," he said.

At his mention of the "beginning," the sadness came over me again as it had in Woodstock. What was it about?

"So it's a way of giving something of the earth back to the earth?" I said.

He nodded. He gently dug a small hole in the earth. Then he raised the tobacco over his head, beckoning to the sky. He repeated this, facing in each of the four cardinal directions, pausing briefly to bow his head respectfully in each direction. After this, he raised the tobacco above his head, then motioned it down over the earth. I thought this to mean he was offering the tobacco to God and then to Mother Earth.

"Grandfather Mountain," he voiced loudly to the sky, "may our Mother give you many children. May the children and the children born from them see with their hearts full. May they come to know, as we have, of the softness of your touch on the path. I call to my relatives, the ancient rock people. You honor us with strong voice. It has shown the way of spirit. It is so."

He placed the tobacco in the hole and refilled it with earth, taking great care to smooth over the surface and not leave a trace of digging.

I heard the words still ringing through the valley. They made my heart soar. I felt the earth under me in a way I had never known before; it supported me. I peered around at the rest of nature. I sensed friends. I felt in some way physically closer to the forest. It was difficult to call up words to describe these feelings to myself. They were foreign to me and, at the same time, right. Yes, right. I had a feeling of rightness. Was that perhaps what spirit was: a feeling of rightness with the world?

"Why did you face in different directions?" I asked.

"To offer blessings and send prayers to the north, east, south, west."

"What do they represent?"

"Much," he said. Then he paused, as if listening for something, and said, "For now let me offer you this, John: Part of what they represent is the four races: north, the white race; east, the yellow race; south, the black race; west, the red race. It is so."

I liked that.

Chapter Six

We headed down the opposite side of the mountain, I assumed in the direction of the lake. At that point, to question where we were heading seemed out of place. The soft glow of twilight was upon us. The terrain on this side was less ferocious and went considerably easier, so we made it down to the bottom quickly. It wasn't really a bottom; the mountain just gracefully moved into the valley. Why had I not seen the transition to the mountain as we went up? I could sense the reason was important but too precious to analyze. Was I learning? Black Hawk was a few steps in front of me as we moved through the fir trees, now looming a deep green all around us. What might he tell me when we reached the place he had spoken of? The place to which spirit, God, would guide us? Why had I so passively accepted his instructions to wait? In Woodstock I thought because I understood intellectually the difference between what he referred to as mind and spirit. But it was just an intellectual understanding which had never done me any good. So what really restrained my questioning?

We had gone about mile when I began to glimpse through the trees small patches of the lake. It looked inviting. I was anxious to get there. Then, simultaneously, we heard a gun shot. Then, quickly, another.

Black Hawk ducked down on his haunches in a flash before the sound of the first shot had even finished. It was a tactical duck, not a panicked one. I followed his lead. The shots seemed to come from in front of us and to the right. I couldn't judge their distance. Another shot. Black Hawk tugged at my sleeve, then began running in a crouched position. I followed. He swept in a wide arc around the apparent path of the bullets. He ran with stealth. His eyes narrowed, almost to slits, and his breathing was extremely deep and evenly paced. I had never seen a human breathe like that. He seemed to breathe with his whole body, much as an animal does.

We ran for fifty yards. Then he stopped and rested his hand on the ground, sensing the hunters' direction from vibrations. Then he peered through the foliage inches above the ground and, satisfied with what he saw, burst ahead for what seemed another calculated fifty yards. He stopped and repeated the process, always in total control.

I assumed from the first shot that it was hunters and was immediately worried about surprising them and getting shot at by accident. But Black Hawk had reacted so quickly that I had no chance to say anything. I thought, wasn't this tactical maneuvering a little much to avoid the possibility of getting hit? After the third reconnaissance stop I asked, "What are we doing? Why don't we yell out to them and tell them we're in the woods?"

The fierce look he gave me left no room for further questioning nor for hope of a response. I was annoyed at his arrogance. What were we doing? I wanted to know. We could get hurt. I've heard of enough foolish and unnecessary hunting accidents.

Another shot. They were getting closer, or we were getting closer to them.

A clump of thick bushes concealed us. Black Hawk stayed very still, again peering through the bushes inches above the ground. I was to his right, nervous. I was afraid to move, knowing a rustling bush was an instant target. But I still wanted to jump up and yell. In a flash of common sense I knew that to surprise them with a yell – as they were perhaps within visual range of us – could be fatally stupid. Everything had happened so quickly. How had I gotten myself into this?

Black Hawk turned his head toward me and, I think, sensed my fear and confusion. He fixed me with a purposeful gaze and stuck two fingers in the air like a peace sign, then he ran that hand, palm turned down, two inches over the ground, gradually sweeping his hand in upward arc. I had no idea what that meant and silently indicated such to him. He repeated the movement and looked off in a direction away from the impending hunters. Did he mean to run?

Then as if appearing out of thin air, a deer of incredible size dashed in front of us, running in the direction Black Hawk had signaled to me. The buck was running so fast he was almost a blur. Black Hawk sprang up and ran at a right angle to the deer's direction, but still away from the hunters. I followed without hesitation. I couldn't see the hunters yet, but heard them clearly. They were shouting back and forth to each other as they hurtled recklessly through the brush. It was an invasive, brutal sound, and I didn't like it.

Black Hawk and I, still crouched, ran fast towards the lake. I kept peering behind me as the shouts and now laughter reached me. Shouts of, "This way. Did you see the size of him?" "I don't care what you say, I spotted him, and he's mine." "Those antlers are going to look good over my fireplace".

It angered me. I still couldn't see them, but they were headed in our direction. It was then I realized what we were doing: We were pulling them off the deer.

A feeling of purpose and quiet surged through me. Like the other feelings I had experienced since meeting Black Hawk, it felt foreign but familiar, natural. But I thought of none of this as we drove through the forest like the wind, like a deer – yes, that's how I felt – like a deer. I never feared tripping or falling or hitting a tree. The perfect path kept unfolding. For a moment, I lost all sense of who I was – who I thought I was.

We weaved through the tightly-bunched trees faster and faster till the shouts behind us became indiscernible. I'm not sure how long or far we ran; it was past any capacity of mine. I felt far from tired; instead I felt elated, as if I had discovered I could fly, and had flown. I was entirely absorbed in the moment, a phenomenon I had known only in childhood. I liked it and wanted more of it.

We came into a natural clearing, and Black Hawk slowed. I, shifted down at the same moment. I listened, to see if we had lost the hunters.

"My brother," Black Hawk said, "darkness has chased them back up the trail." He outlined night falling with a graceful hand, then swept it back towards the beginning of our flight. A feeling of softness came into my chest.

"It is good," he said. "Tunkashila honors us by bringing us to a place of power. John, see the circle made by the Grandfather Trees?"

"Yes," I answered. It was a natural circle. Before I inquired on the significance, he was ahead of me, as always.

"The circle represents much, like the four directions." He smiled the smile again, and the good student smiled in return to indicate understanding. He continued. "For now, you are born, you die. All life returns from where it began. The spirit returns to Tunkashila. It is so."

Fairly simple. I thought I got it.

He sat down cross-legged in what looked to be precisely the center of the circle and motioned me quite grandly – but somehow humbly, as well – to sit across from him. I did so. He took a long moment in quiet. The moon cast a soft light over the circle. Then my attention was caught by Black Hawk's eyes piercing me. He sat two feet from me but it seemed inches, as he held my eyes in a grip.

"These hunters have much anger inside, John. They say they hunt for meat, but what they hunt are their feelings – their feelings of anger for others, for themselves." He sketched the picture with his hands, passion mounting.

"They walk by Grandfather Tree and upon our Mother, the Earth, with anger in their hearts. These hunters take this anger and turn it against all; they use it on the four-legged, on the winged, on Mother Earth. Then their mind says, 'See, I am more powerful.'

"Before I meet my brother the deer, he is already part of me, his spirit is part of my spirit. I offer many prayers for him, dance and sing in honor of his spirit, and ask that his journey to Tunkashila may be that of a warrior. He gives of himself so that I may feed my family and keep the winter wind from passing through. It is so."

I sat with my back straight, listening to his words. They carried such power; I could see him offering prayers to honor the deer, then how he would stalk through the woods, come upon the deer, and take him with honor.

"John, we have come to the path that tells how I came to Woodstock and how you and I now walk as warriors together."

"This is the place?" I asked.

"We have come to the place of spirit in you, John."

"You mean there isn't a real place?"

He shook his head.

Then I got it. I had to find the place of spirit in me.

"Have I?" I asked him.

He pointed his two fingers like a peace sign, then ran the flat of that handover the ground, sweeping upwards. I watched the movement, then looked into his face. It was filled with pride, and I knew. Nothing more needed to be said. He spoke of my act in joining him to pull the hunters from the deer.

I sat with my head high, feeling a bond with this stranger, a bond imbued with a sense of dignity, as well as near sadness, bitter sweetness. I wanted to express this, but there were no words to fit how I felt. So I remained still until he clenched his two fists in front his chest, and said, "It is good."

He seemed to listen for something inside again. Then he began. "Many seasons ago, the moon was in its last quarter, as it is now. Many brave warriors sat beside me in the circle of life. We sang to the Great Spirit to bless our hunt, for it was the time to hunt the great buffalo. Many prayers were offered as the Grandfather Tree gave us the light to fill the circle. The old ones began to beat the sacred drum, beating as our heart beats. Those who carried the sacred song from their fathers sang of the hunt. The Great Spirit called to me. I answered, singing with a voice that was not of my own, but of Tunkashila's. It swept through the night over the heart of Mother Earth, reaching above to Grandfather Sky and His many eyes. My voice was true and strong. I remember not the words. Song and music, John, are the essence of the spirit. It is our way to thank Tunkashila for what he has given. It is much. Then before me, John, a vision appeared, a vision of a gathering of many nations of all races, from the four directions – white, black, yellow, red. This gathering lasted three days."

A chill went through me.

"A gathering that spoke of future, for it was of spirit. Spirit is of the future. Young and old sat as one in a great council, hearing the song and music that spoke of freedom, of love – paths of spirit.

"Tunkashila blessed them with the rains, for water is cleansing and of new life. It was good. My heart was full.

"But then my vision turned to the east, to the yellow race, where a war of mind was fought for many seasons. A war that was kept on the earth by few, for mazaska, money. Many warriors, on both sides, fought and died bravely. Their death came into the hearts of the young, joining them into one nation. This nation's voice spoke above others, quieting the shouts of the dying. It was good, for many could see the power of spirit. For who is it who gives us spirit? It is Tunkashila. Tunkashila is not of war. When spirit speaks through mind, it brings power, brings knowing. But many take another road, the road of mind speaking through spirit. This road is of fear.

"The vision spoke of a time of great leaders. A man of the black race, of the south, who joined his nation together as one to journey on a great road of spirit. The road was perilous. Many wished to destroy it, many who had been taught from when they were young to fear other races. But they did not see that they could not destroy the road. For the road of spirit was in each man. What is more powerful? The road of God or the road of fear that is created by man? It was so. Freedom was seen in the eyes of all. When the leader of these people met death, he met death as a great warrior. The people saw the road they walked. They saw that it was true and strong, and they were of God. It was the beginning, not the end."

I tried to interpret what he was saying.

"A man of the white race, of strong voice and strong spirit spoke to the nations of the earth. A tall man. His vision was of the future, of men walking softly on the earth in peace, together. He spoke of how each man must choose spirit and not wait for spirit to choose him. His vision of the future was also feared by many. He died as a great warrior on his journey of the spirit. All honored his spirit.

"In this time, man created a great fire to harm Mother Earth. A fire made by man, not Tunkashila. It is so. All feared this great fire.

"I saw that upon the earth, tall stone and metal structure stood harming the earth, taking life from it. John, the earth lives as we do. I saw the great waters of the east and west in darkness for the light could not come through. I saw many Grandfather Trees cut from the earth before it was time. I saw the four-legged, the winged, the fish, my brothers, my sisters, and your brothers and sisters, who are all part of the great circle of life, being taken from the circle.

"I saw that many fought as warriors during this time. They gathered in great numbers as one to speak out against these fears. Their heart was strong. Their voice raised high and was heard by Tunkashila, and knowing lived.

"The vision talked of many of these things – of a leader of the white people who feared his people and left the path of honor. It spoke of the need of money, of the need to be better than the brothers and sisters of other races. It spoke of how many live from mind, not heart. For it is a heart they have built great walls around.

"My vision returned to the great gathering of many nations which covered the land like the great buffalo. I saw you, John, at this place. Your spirit was strong."

What did he mean, he "saw" me?

"You went from this gathering and soon silenced your spirit. Your mind spoke to you. You lived with fear and sought not spirit but money. But your spirit is strong, like many of that time. It called to you. But the path was not clear, so you returned to the place called Woodstock."

I was becoming frightened now. I tried to speak, but he silenced me with a wave of his hand.

"John, here in Woodstock, you have lived of mind. You know of this, for your spirit speaks. But you turn your back. As I saw you in the center on your place where you have remained for many seasons, my vision gave its last breath.

"Tunkashila had told me much. The gift was great. I stood and danced in thanks. The dance was given to me by my spirit brother, the hawk. I could hear the drumming and the singing of my brothers, the Sioux. I danced, giving all of me. Tunkashila whispered to me that I must show you the path of no words. I called to the hawk. He came to me and we walked the wind to a place called Woodstock. It is so. For I am Black Hawk Who Walks the Wind. A Ho."

Walked the wind? What was he talking about? It made no sense. Was it some kind of metaphor?

"I'm not sure I know what you mean by walking the wind."

He responded with the utmost slowness, his eyes boring into me. "John, it is a time that has not yet come for me."

"What do you mean?" I asked.

"My time is many seasons ago."

"I'm not following you," I said.

He peered into my eyes, and for a fleeting moment I saw not his face but the face of a hawk. It frightened me. I started fidgeting and kept my eyes riveted to the ground in fear of seeing it again.

"All is possible, John."

"What is possible?" I snapped.

"What you have just seen."

"What are you talking about?" My hands trembled. He didn't answer. After a painfully long moment, I looked directly at him and jumped up, backing away in fright. I again saw the hawk's face, the hawk's black eyes boring into me.

Then, flatly, with absolute unbending conviction, he said, "John, I am from the past."

"What?!" The dark woods closed in. I was suddenly trapped. I felt the door to a cell slam shut.

"Two hundred and thirty years ago in your language. Tunkashila has spoken that you have the power to see what I speak of – to see." He embellished the phrase with the powerful gesture of moving two fingers away from his eyes.

"I have journeyed into the future – your time. We call it dreaming. I call to my brother the hawk and we become one, the same spirit." With slow grace, he placed two index fingers side by side.

I was frozen in place several feet from him.

"We travel the wind, my relative, for the wind is my brother and supports and protects me. The wind is...special to me," he said, reaching for the English of the adverb.

"As you, too, have relatives that are always near to help you on your journey."

"You're telling me that you're from 1700's?" I yelled.

"It is so."

"How do you expect me to believe such a thing?"

"Look inside, it will always give you what you need. Have the will to know what is there for you to see."

Have the will, I thought. Isn't that what the problem has always been? I felt so tired, so very tired. The years and years of defeat and not getting what I wanted in life crashed down on me. I held the tears back with the little strength I had left.

"What does having the will have to do with it?!"

"It lets us see what we want to see."

Those words reached deep inside and silenced me. I was angry at the way he could affect me. I tried desperately to sustain the anger. It was the only thing that stood between us now, the only thing left to shield me from freedom.

"Look, I have no idea what you're talking about," I said.

He didn't respond, but just looked at me with those black eyes – fierce and proud. He was communicating something to me…a feeling…I recognized it then: honor. I suddenly felt that place inside me. I remembered the place where I had stood with dignity, with pride. I saw how my words of doubt and anger have no place beside the actions of a warrior. I raised my hand and greeted him, "A Ho."

Chapter Seven

We built a fire. For the first time I saw one lit without matches. He had placed a stick upright on a flat wood surface and spun it between his palm still a spark flashed. Then he fed thin brush to the spark and it became a tiny flame, then a fire. Independence.

The fire was small but gave off a good amount of light. We sat watching, mesmerized by the flames, for some time. I was reminded of camping trips when I was a kid and how we'd sat for hours staring into the fire, imagining all sorts of things; never being able to get quite close enough to the dancing flames.

The silence of the woods surrounded Black Hawk and me. I could live my life in this silence, this peace. Words seemed only to confuse things.

"I say Ho to you, my relative." Black Hawk spoke suddenly, holding his hand close to the fire. "It is with one spark that the fire begins. It is with one spark that the fire is born from the womb of Mother Earth and grows strong. It is with one spark that the white fire, the yellow fire, red and black fires, join as one, one spirit." He pointed toward the different colors in the flames. "Let the fire of the Sacred Hoop grow strong, grow high, grow as one blue fire, the spirit light, the light of Tunkashila. Let one spirit reach high to you, Grandfather Sky. If I can offer but one spark, Tunkashila, Ho."

The fire blazed higher with these words, and the flames, as he said, united into one color, blue.

"One spark, John. Hold this in your heart."

I nodded solemnly. We lapsed back into silence. I thought back on my search for wood. I had ventured by myself into the interior of the forest, a bit past where the light stopped. After my eyes had adjusted to the dark, I could see fairly well and that feeling of sensing friends close by had come to me again. I had wanted to sit down against a tree for a spell and enjoy the solitude, but thoughts of "can't do that, I might miss something" had rushed into my head. I recognized those thoughts right away. For years I had observed the way they plagued me and fenced me in. But my observation had never turned to action.

Suddenly, there in the woods, I had a bit of clarity and thought, I am going to give myself this little enjoyment. So I sat down against a big elm tree. I didn't see or hear Black Hawk; he had gone off in the opposite direction.

I peered around and thought, I am by myself. That comforted me. The quiet of the woods swept through me, gentling me inside. I felt safe. I took in the different-colored leaves that lay around me and how trees were given life from the earth.

I was brought suddenly back to what Black Hawk had said about the earth being our Mother, and I felt I knew what he meant. It was a knowing that was changing my perception of the earth.

Then I realized I had given no thought to his extraordinary statements about being from the past or to the hawk I had seen superimposed on his face. Maybe part of me wanted to believe – desperately to believe – all was possible.

I had a sudden urge to run through the nearly pitch-black woods. I felt myself wanting to let go and recapture the feeling I'd had when we ran from the hunters. I sensed independence and freedom waiting out there among the trees.

I must have hesitated too long. Thoughts crept in: it was too dark; I would run head-on into a skull-splitting tree; I might trip over a big rock, smashing my nose into the ground. So I walked out of the woods with my armful of wood, though every few steps I felt the urge, the need, to fly through the trees. Once I looked behind me into the dark forest and imagined myself weaving through the trees, knowing my feet would find a clear path as long as I trusted. But again, my head got in the way, with nonsense about getting hurt and so on and so on. I returned to the circle, feeling I had left an opportunity behind.

Now the fire blazed between us. How different the world must be on his side of the flames. It was only on the other side, a few feet from me. But how did it differ? He interrupted my speculations, knowingly, I think!

"John, what do you need to feel right?" His use of

"right" surprised me; it sounded out of place coming from him. But it was accurate.

"What do I need? Wait a minute, let me find my list. I need to find a way out of where I am, this place I've been stuck in for years. Hell, too many years!"

"Do you want change?"

"Yes, of course I do," I half yelled.

"You have seen change in your time, as my vision spoke of, is this not so?"

"That's right. Your vision talked about the time of the sixties when we felt we could affect things, that the individual could make a difference. We were going to change the world. I think you meant the Vietnam war, and we, the people, stopped that war, just as your vision said. And leaders like King and Kennedy, they moved a whole nation, a whole world, to believe that we could fight oppression, that we could have a voice. I just don't know what happened. Somewhere along the way, after the concert at Woodstock, I lost it.

"I tell you, I will never forget those three days. They were so full of love and possibility. Yes, that was it: possibility."

"Do you fear the possibility of change?" he asked.

"No, why would I fear it?"

"Then why is it you do not see that it is possible?"

"Because...I don't know."

"Hear me now, John, for these words are of Tunkashila. The people of Woodstock, of that time, saw the future. They had a dream, and that dream was coming. They felt fear because they saw they could make a change, they could a make a difference. They saw they had a power over themselves, but they asked, What do we do with this power? Do we want this change? It was so much easier when somebody else told us what to do and when to do it.

"To change is to let oneself go to spirit, not just to talk about believing in God or about believing in oneself, but to live that belief each and every day."

I sat there in shock. I knew immediately what he said to be true. But so embarrassingly simple. Nobody had come along and said, "Time's up, turn in your equipment, the Movement is over."

"You're right, absolutely right," I said. "I don't know when I decided it was easier to live by the rules. I guess it doesn't matter now. I don't know about my friends, but that is surly what I did. Maybe I knew it all along.

"If we claimed our own power, then nobody was to blame but ourselves. We would have to take responsibility for our world, our lives. Because we would know. Once you know, there is no turning back, no getting away with the same old nonsense of blaming life on others. Is that why I was so unhappy all those years? The sixties taught me about my own power as a human being. Then I ran from it. But the track I ran on was mined with conscience and judgment, vultures sitting above me saying, 'You know better, it's too late.'"

We laughed.

"John," Black Hawk said, "we must let our roots grow deep into Mother Earth. Look at that tree that reaches high, the old tree that has grown its roots deep. It stands tall and touches Tunkashila. But the tree that rushes its growth and makes a shallow base, what will become of it? The first big wind will push it over. And that's what your people have done. They don't root themselves in the earth first. They don't appreciate the earth for what it is. They don't believe it is a living thing. They must touch the earth. To touch the earth is to appreciate your Mother, your true Mother. For it is she who keeps me alive. It is the She who kept my mother alive."

"What do you mean, root ourselves in Mother Earth?"

"The roots must be deep," he said. "Before a child runs, it must crawl. In the beginning the way may be lined with thorn bushes. Everything has its opposite. There is good, there is bad; there is light, there is darkness; there is death, there is life. As we walk, we will meet opposites. To know pain, to know suffering, is to know when the dream has come. If it is good, of value, it will take time.

"It is all a test of your spirit," he said, "to bring it strength, to make you strong. In these tests, we are forced to choose and learn.

"Each moment can be a test when we open ourselves to spirit and choose to walk that road. Listen closely: Those who choose this road have called spirit on to the field of battle. It is only in the choosing that we travel forward on the road to Tunkashila. Do you see?"

"No, not quite," I said.

"You feel many years have been lost, not so?"

"Yes, exactly, I feel they've been wasted."

"When you choose again to walk the path of spirit, will hardship and defeat have made you stronger, made you appreciate more the good that comes to you?"

"Yes, I guess, but I still don't see what you're getting at."

"Only when you walk on the path again do those years give you strength."

"So my past only changes when my purpose does?"

He nodded. "Can you see now, on this day, what you have learned in the many seasons since the gathering at Woodstock?"

"After the concert, I worked for the system I had fought. Then I ran to Woodstock, hoping to find something. But I was miserable. I am miserable! I judge everything and everyone, including myself. I tell you, I've learned where the answers aren't. No matter what you do, you can never escape yourself. But you see, even knowing this has done me no good. And I'm sure I'm not alone on this. The last two generations have sought spirituality, have sought some happiness. They have struggled with the frustration of knowing that intellectual understanding of all the philosophies in the universe is of absolutely no value. After a while I too learned it was of no value. But I continued intellectualizing, and doing it in misery; a misery I protected and fought to keep intact."

"Today have you seen the beauty of the earth and the many gifts she has given?" he asked.

"Yes. Maybe I wouldn't have appreciated it as much if I hadn't struggled for so long – even if the struggle was internal, against myself. Each moment of each day the door to freedom loomed in front of me, condemning me, always, for not opening it.

"But why," I wondered aloud, "why did I come with you today? This is what I don't understand. It's as if I had made a decision without knowing it. It doesn't make any sense."

"You must not question the path of spirit, John, the path of God. Does it feel right inside?"

"Yes, it does."

"This is all that is needed. Ho"

"It's as if I recognized – yes, that's it," I said, "I had recognized a part of you in me. Why do I feel that way?"

"We are all of the same spirit."

"Yes, I know, but I think that recognition is what made me accept that you're from the past. Why? Why did this recognition lead to decisions, to trust?"

"All thoughts are shadow, John. They cannot lead you to a place of freedom. No matter how important, how bright they look."

"I still don't understand what defines walking the path of spirit, but in some strange way I feel as though I do know. I can't put it into words. I've heard of this infliction before and have always resented it. Well, at least I'll no longer do that."

We laughed.

"Will I always have to struggle to learn something?" I asked.

"We are warriors and have called spirit into battle," he said with pride. "It is a battle with no enemy, no victor, no loser. There is only knowing."

"Is knowing a feeling of instinct, of understanding the truth? A feeling of freedom?"

He grinned. "Words have no spirit, John. Talking here" – he swept his hand in front of him, then touched his temples – "and here. When we stand as warriors and walk the path of spirit, then spirit will find us, not words."

I started to rub the headache I was getting.

"Listen with spirit, good healer," he offered with a laugh.

"Thanks. I still don't understand what it means to listen with spirit. I feel as though I've experienced it, but I couldn't do it on command. I know what it isn't – to listen with the intellect, the mind. It isn't something tangible. But when I'm listening from that place, I know it. I can feel it. How do you do it, listen with spirit?!"

He took a moment, listening inside for something.

"Words have no spirit, John." Again he swept his hand in front of him and again lightly touched his temples.

"Yes, I know, I got that." I heard the infamous "I know" come out of my mouth, and cringed. I was always pinning people on their overuse of "I know."

"Then why do you seek words?"

"I know, I know." There it was again! "It's just, how can I understand it if you don't explain it to me?"

The damn smile again.

"I hear what you're trying to say," I said, "but still I don't see how I can begin to..." I gave up and shook my head in frustration. I tried to communicate a silent, "give me break, I'm just a poor helpless product of my environment." He laughed and offered a morsel of riddle-wisdom.

"Spirit never loses its way."

"That's it?! Thanks. I forgot what I was trying to listen for anyway. What happened here? I thought I was starting to make progress. I'm confused and need an aspirin. Aren't the details a way at getting at the answers?"

His only response was the "look."

"Won't the details help me know how to be happy or at least what was making me unhappy? If I knew, I wouldn't do it any more, right? Aren't my questions an attempt or indication that I really want to learn to be a better person? I'm being as honest as I can. Aren't I confronting my faults?"

This induced laughter in Black Hawk. In a few seconds, it evolved into a full-blown rolling back and forth on the ground.

"You having a good time?" I inquired.

"John, what is it that you fear not knowing?"

"Everything!"

"This is what I thought! How do you know what is on the other side of the stream, till you step in the water and cross?"

"Good question."

"Could get wet, but it's part of our journey. Knowing comes from action. Words, John, mean nothing. Fear of trusting – "He spread his hands to the sky, to God." The mind says there is an easier way. Words have no power without spirit, only shadow." He touched his temples again. Why did he keep doing this? I knew he meant the conversation we get into with ourselves, and I had been indicating my understanding with a continual exaggerated and perfectly effected nod. His use of the word "shadow" was interesting, and I had begun to ask him about it when he intercepted me.

"Let your mind feel the quiet of a morning breeze."

I was solemn but I understood. He meant for me to quiet my thoughts. But my understanding was intellectual, as it had been for years.

"It just doesn't work. I can't get my head out of the way. I can't translate what I understand up here into action. It doesn't change anything."

"Words can never tell you of what I speak."

I retreated into silence, weary of my own voice. A moment later, I found him gazing up at the sky. There was a slightly mischievous smile on his face. He seemed very focused and didn't return my gaze for a long moment, then turned and smiled at me. It was an innocent child's smile. I smiled back. Suddenly, a powerful, warm wind rushed over us for about ten seconds, then stopped. It was as if a person had run by. The sound of it passing through the trees warmed my heart and made my smile deepen.

"The wind has offered its agreement," he said.

I grinned, not really taking him seriously. I stayed still within that feeling of quiet and warmth, just enjoying it, thinking of nothing for a minute or two. The details of my interrogation dissolved. Then, suddenly, I GOT IT! – KNOWING CAME FROM A FEELING, CAME THROUGH A FEELING. THAT WAS IT! Every time I truly felt I understood something in a deeper, instinctual way, saw it with true clarity, it was communicated THROUGH a feeling. Like when I was searching for wood and suddenly understood about the earth being our Mother. That knowing came through a feeling of quiet, of security, of goodness. They were all feelings of love. Spirit was simply love.

Elation rushed through me in a physical jolt. I wanted to jump up, run around, and shout with joy. But I hesitated. Suddenly, the wind returned. I recognized it; it was the same wind I had felt just before I met Black Hawk. It blew across my face, and I let go. I jumped up, ran around with my hands over my head in a victory dance of some sort. The wind blew stronger and stronger matching the surge of joy in me. The warm gusts encircled me, pushing me from all sides. I felt it healing the hurts inside me, making me stronger. I was lost in joy. I staggered to a stop. I knew what I had to do. I raised my open hands to the sky and said, "Thank you for this gift."

Then I stood perfectly still and looked around as the wind blew over me. I felt a part of each star, each tree, each granule of earth under me. I felt a simplicity I wanted never to go away. Every agonizing, suffering moment I had ever experienced was worth it to reach this place. Life was truly a gift.

Then the wind just stopped, I looked over at Black Hawk, who sat with his back straight, head high. He said, "John, you should make an offering of tobacco for the gift of spirit that has been given to you."

"Okay. Will you show me how, what to say?"

"I cannot speak what is in your heart. Only you can do this."

He handed me the deerskin pouch. I sensed something

sacred lying inside and I was nervous, tentative, as I opened it. Black Hawk watched me with an expression of knowing and, also, surprise; I wondered what that look was about.

My fingers reached in and touched the small leaves. I felt an immediate urge to hold a handful, and I did. The tobacco felt a part of me, alive and precious. I brought the handful against my chest. I held it there, not wanting to let the small handful go.

"The wind is your relative as it is mine, a powerful relative," Black Hawk said.

I pondered that for a moment, then took a couple of steps away and raised my hands, with the tobacco in one of them, over my head. The simple words came to me then, filled with a sincerity that for once didn't feel manipulated.

"Tunkashila, God, thank you for this great gift, this gift of understanding, this gift of knowing. I offer this to you in thanks. Spirit of the wind, my brother, thank you for your strength and guidance. I offer this to you in thanks."

The wind suddenly came up again. I knelt, dug out a small hole in the earth with my fingers, and placed the tobacco in it. Then I filled in the hole, gently patting the surface. I held my hand protectively over the spot for a few seconds. The wind continued to blow. A thought came to me. I raised another bit of tobacco over my head, then opened my hand. The wind swept the tiny leaves away. I closed my eyes and an insight suddenly pierced through all my frames of reference and imbedded itself inside the silence within me. It was an insight different than any other I had received in my life – I knew it was a fact.

I turned to Black Hawk and whispered, "You don't have to do anything."

"Ho, Tunkashila," he responded.

I understood for the first time why he could not, and would not, give me the full explanations I had pleaded for. Words were not adequate. They had too many associations for me. The truth could be only communicated through a feeling. It was the feeling of love which penetrated my belief systems.

"You don't have to do anything," showed me how I had spent a lifetime doing things to myself. I was always up in my head doing something – assessing, judging, analyzing, labeling, categorizing, justifying, associating, resenting, envying, hating – an endless list. Also, to round that off, I was trying not to do those things, or in other words, doing "not doing." In fact, I saw how I'd been "doing" with Black Hawk's words throughout the day.

When I found spirit, there were no questions. I saw the world clearly. I saw the naturally good person I am and found the ease to act as such. Stop doing so much and just be. You don't have to do anything, I told myself, because you are naturally wise – just give the mind a rest, and this wisdom you crave will show itself – and you will act upon it.

I laughed to think of how hard I had resisted books that spoke about truth being inside. It was as much a part of us as our eyes, our ears, and our hearts.

I wanted to tell Black Hawk all of this, but he fixed my eyes with his own. He turned his left palm down, and forcefully pushed it toward me. "John," he asked, "when you reach other side of stream, do you remain there or move up path?"

"I guess I would keep walking."

"It is so."

"What are you saying?"

"Even the gifts of spirit knowledge should not be held, should not be spoken, before the roots are deep."

"How can I put into my life what I've learned if I don't hold on to it? Why can't I talk about it?"

"All life is of spirit. You cannot hold spirit with words; only by remaining on the path of no words."

"I know. I understand now what you've been trying to tell me about spirit, and how words mean nothing," I said. "But what are you getting at?"

"Spirit cannot be found or lost. You have learned this."

Had I? Why was I getting so upset over this? Was I defending my insight? Why? Maybe I was holding on to it. I couldn't seem to win a round here! He seemed to know right where my weaknesses were.

He raised his two fingers to his eyes and swept them toward me. "You must see what there is to see."

Chapter Eight

I sat back down across from him, and he resumed immediately. "John, the eyes of spirit can see much that is hidden from our mind. They can see the innocence of those who do not follow the path of spirit, those who do not listen when spirit speaks to them of right or wrong. For that is what part of spirit is – the voice inside each man or woman that whispers to them."

The eyes of spirit see the innocence of fear that we carry on our backs. Fear, John, you have carried heavy on your back. You must see with innocence your own fear. Here are the words of Tunkashila, for they are good."

"What do you mean, carry on my back?"

He laughed.

"When we are sick, we pray to Tunkashila for strength and healing. Do we pray when our body and spirit are strong?"

"I don't know, I'm a bit new at this."

We laughed. It felt good.

"Spirit, power, knowing are all the same. Seek these when strong, not when weak."

"I'm still not getting it. What does that have to do with me carrying fear on my back?" I asked.

"You must remember I have not answered some of the questions you have asked. I answer to your spirit, not your mind. These words test your spirit. I am not here to help your mind, but your spirit on your earth-walk. That is what belongs to your Father and my Father." He smiled, and tapped my head.

"Oh no, I did it again. You're right! How could I do it after all that."

"Innocence," he said flatly.

"Innocence? Mmm. Okay, let's go back one more time to seeking knowing when strong."

"Knowing, wisdom, come to you through feeling of love, through feeling when spirit is full inside. It is not so?"

"Yeah." I was solemn and a bit hesitant.

"But when we are right with the earth and it provides us with shelter and food, do we seek knowing, do we seek to deepen the roots of our spirit? No. Only when we become sick or our heart is in shadow do we ask for help from Tunkashila. Then we cannot hear, for only the mind hears. Do you see, John?"

"You mean that true knowledge can only be absorbed through a positive feeling, a feeling of love, of spirit. But we never think of seeking wisdom when we feel good, when we feel right with the world. We only want wisdom when things are not going well. And then we can't hear because we're depressed. Our minds are filled with negativity and defenses, all armed for attack and capture. But how do I get back to feeling positive? Especially when I thought I'd broken through to some truths."

He was silent a moment. Then an enormous grin spread across his face. He was barely able to hold his laughter in.

"Do you want to let me in on it?" I inquired.

"When I was young, I lost my way in the woods," he told me. "Many days passed – four, five moons. I saw signs that death was close. In my dying, I knew that all would be shown to me…I knew but I kept my eyes open all night."

He opened his eyes wide, like a frightened child.

"I thought I saw death in the trees, in the bushes. I prayed to spirits to protect me, prayed with great voice, much feeling. Soon the sun came, and death had not taken me!"

He collapsed with laughter. So did I. Then, gasping, he composed himself and resumed.

"I heard through the trees the calls of my father. I ran toward his voice. I fell and hit my head on a big rock. Light turned to black. Then I saw many people, strangers, in the darkness. They spoke to the heart, with no words. But my heart was closed with fear and much anger, for I thought I had gone to other world."

More laughs.

"In that other world there was no light, only shadows, big like the Great Grandfather Tree. The shadows spoke to me of past and future as if they were not separate. I yelled at the shadows: This is wrong, I am dead; living is my past. The shadows puffed up bigger and stood over me, laughing big laughs. I ran, but they chased me, leaned closer and laughed louder. I decided to run no longer. I remembered I was a warrior; I must face them. I stopped and turned. The shadows were gone. I searched everywhere, but the shadows were not hiding. I sat down, and the ground felt soft. I felt safe in the place of darkness. The darkness became friend. I saw that darkness was a place of light. It is so."

He finished the tale with the grin of a satisfied woodnymph. We laughed.

"Laughter is also part of spirit, isn't it?" I asked. "I remember that during the day when my mind was racing with a hundred details and worries, we'd laugh and suddenly the worries were forgotten. My need for answers and conclusions had disappeared."

"Ho," he responded.

Chapter Nine

We heard the hoot of owls and the scurry of small animals in the brush as we watched our shadows, cast by the fire, stretch to the tops of trees. I felt us touching all life; we were not alone.

Black Hawk continued. "Future, John, has come and has gone. It is never where you think it will be. Future belongs to those who walk straight and feel the earth under them. If we can find the future of ourselves, we have seen all that is good, all that is of God."

"What does that mean?!" Wait, I thought, hadn't I grasped how to listen?

"Sorry, I guess my arsenal of reactions are coming out one by one. The troops!"

"It is all a test of your spirit to bring it strength, to make you strong. In these tests we are forced to choose and learn."

"There is a choice, isn't there? I could try to figure out what you mean, or I could just have faith that it will reveal itself in its own time."

"You will see, John."

I nodded solemnly.

Then a darkness descended over me. How far I was from comprehending the unknowns of life. Perhaps Black Hawk shared my sudden change of mood. He turned a palm down and traced an arc that encompassed the horizon.

He said with sadness, "This time is distant from heart."

He gazed out at the rows of trees guarding us and listened. The sadness left his face and was replaced by purpose. "We must make a Sacred Hoop."

"How do we do that?"

"John, you find a branch on the ground by the Grandfather Tree. Then we make Sacred Hoop," he said.

"Just any branch?"

"You will see the branch." He conveyed a faith-smile.

I walked some twenty feet from the fire to the tree line, and peered into the dense forest. This time there was no whisper of welcome from the dark web of sinewy bushes and trees. I rechecked Black Hawk's distance from me. It appeared to be several miles, out of shouting-for-help range from attacks from double-bladed-axe-flesh eaters! I began to compose an excuse of why I chose a branch from the perimeter and not the woods. Then I thought, no, returning with an transparent excuse was much worse than anything I could encounter a few steps into the trees. Finally I crossed the line. A dark impenetrable wall rose up, and my foot disappeared in front of me. Even the trees were no longer in shadowy outline. How, I wondered, had I seen clearly earlier? But I stopped wondering in the interest of getting out quickly.

I walked forward tentatively into what appeared to be an opening between shrubs and branches. Out of the darkness, an eye-gouging tentacle grabbed my face.

"Shi-i-i-t." I blundered forward, further into the woods. I tried to turn my head to see how far behind me the monster was, but my neck seemed frozen.

When I thought I had gained a safe lead, I ducked behind a wide tree which I hoped provided me safety from a rear attack. Then, imagining my throat being ripped open any second, I hunched down. I checked around, and then let out a laugh and said to myself, "There's nothing out here in the dark – but what is that THING WITH AN AXE STANDING OVER THERE?!" I felt like a little kid with his eyes glued on the closet door. I laughed again. A bit schizo here, John. Then suddenly, his words, "carrying fear on my back," came to me through the laugh, through the feeling. I understood in a deeper, clearer way, what he had meant. I chose to feel fear, to carry it. One second, there were man-eaters, and the next, shadows. What changed in the space between those seconds? Not a metamorphosing monster, but me.

I began to see those simple conclusions as facts, facts which were common sense. I saw the implications in my daily life. Perhaps I was beginning to understand the principal of fear via my thinking. Like math, if you comprehended the principal of how to solve a problem, you translated it to answering all similar problems.

From my trust in him, I followed instructions, let go of

these insights, and let the good feelings prevail.

My neck unhinged, and I looked around. My friends the trees were back. I suppose I was back too. I glanced to my right and saw an odd branch laying there. It was curved in a zig-zag shape, like a snake, about three feet long, an inch thick. I picked it up and a warm tangible sensation flowed into my body. The branch appeared a separate entity; the ends didn't seem broken off from a bigger limb. I caught myself sensing all this, then laughed – this was the branch.

With branch in hand, I began to walk out through the trees. Before I re-entered the circle, I faced the forest, raised the branch and said, "Thank you, Grandfather Tree, for this gift. I will honor it as you have honored me." These were foreign words to me, and as I spoke them I felt not myself, not the person I knew. Then the sadness was on me. Why was this? I felt in some way closer to knowing.

I approached Black Hawk and thrust the branch forward and up as if it were an object of power or a weapon raised in celebration. I continued to act in ways that were foreign to me. Perhaps I acted without a thought. I handed the branch to Black Hawk. He examined it, nodded and smiled. I had done well.

Black Hawk used the branch to etch, with deliberate accuracy, a fifteen-foot circle in the ground around the fire. Then one line horizontally down the center, cutting the circle in half, and one line vertically across the center, dividing the circle into four equal parts.

"Why did you draw the two lines?" I asked.

"The four quarters are the four directions, the four races. In the center, is Mother Earth, green. You will sit in the north, the place of the white race, and I in the west, the place of the red race. Now, we go to the lake to prepare ourselves."

"Prepare ourselves? For what?"

He directed those dark eyes, again fierce, at me. I knew that whatever it was, it would be the act of a warrior, an act of honor, for goodness.

Chapter Ten

I kept close behind Black Hawk in the dark woods. He found a clear path and seemed to know exactly where we were going. About two hundred and fifty yards later, much closer than I had thought, the lake revealed itself. It was about two miles across, and the full moon clearly illuminated each shore.

We came into a small clearing right on the edge of the water. Black Hawk took a bit of tobacco out of the pouch and spoke. "Water, blood of Mother Earth, cleanse my brother and me, so that we may enter the Sacred Hoop. Blood of Mother Earth, be there for my relatives, the two-legged, four-legged, and winged, and for those that swim in water, for those that crawl and slither upon the earth, and for those that live inside the womb of Mother Earth. Be there, blood of Mother Earth, for the grandfathers and grandmothers, fathers and mothers, for the children, and for those unborn of all my relatives. Your blood gives the body and spirit the nourishment it needs. A Ho."

Black Hawk leaned out and rested the tobacco on the

lake surface. Then he began to undress.

"Black Hawk, what are we doing?"

He laughed. "We must purify ourselves in the water before we return to the Sacred Hoop."

"You mean go in the water?"

"Yeah!" It was a perfect imitation of me.

"I mean, don't you think it's kind of cold?"

"No more, no more!"

"Okay, OKAY. You want me to go in the water." I began to rip off my clothes.

"Are you sure, John, it's really cold?!"

"Look, I'm going in. All right?"

"Okay, but keep eyes open for man-eating beavers."

"What!?"

He chomped his teeth like a beaver. Then seeing my lack of humor, stamped around in imitation of a man-eating beaver searching for prey. I let out a tiny laugh and imitated his imitationc of carnivorous beavers. Soon we were both cracking up.

Black Hawk calmed down and grew serious. "John, we must enter the water with respect. We will honor the lake, and it will honor us. It is so."

I nodded.

He entered the lake gently, stepping off the short grassy bank into knee-high water. He waded on, barely causing a ripple, until the water reached his waist.

I followed his example, taking great care not to disturb the surface. I got both feet in and stood for a short moment on the muddy bottom. The water caressed me, soothed me.

I felt suddenly calmer and centered. I waded over to him.

We looked across the mirror like surface to the opposite shore. The water was warm, and I pondered that the air must be barely fifty degrees. What a silly thing to question, I thought. Would I prefer to be freezing?

"John," Black Hawk said, "all is safe when we respect all that has been given us. It is given us," he repeated. There was a terrible sadness in his eyes that pierced me. An old anger flared in me, a tremendous need to do something, anything to make it right again, to wake people up. Hell, to wake myself up.

Black Hawk pointed across the lake. "John, look, tell me where you see that it is not possible to change."

"I don't know what you mean."

Then he said ominously, with the proud warrior voice I'd come to recognize, "John, swim out as far as you can." His eyes held mine. My face darkened with an unknown intent. What was it a reaction to, I wondered. I simply felt it. Fierceness of emotion was new to me.

Then he strengthened his words by thrusting his turned down palm toward the center of the lake.

As with the branch, my response came from a person I didn't know. I slowly brought my two index fingers together, holding them side by side, then pushed both my palms face down toward the far shore. He followed my hands, then our eyes met. I felt tears in my eyes, and I saw the sparkle in his. We stood as warriors. Without another motion, we began ever so gently to swim toward the center--together.

I thought of the old man facing Black Hawk in Woodstock. They had exchanged this feeling, where histories, battles, victories, and defeats were all contained. How could words, no matter how eloquent, speak of the depth of these acts. How could they speak of our lifetime, our lifetime within?

I knew, as I think Black Hawk did, that it might be a fatal swim, given the distance and temperature, and I remembered the lesson from the mountain about dying on a journey of spirit. I felt proud I would give myself in such a way. I knew then that what mattered was to speak with spirit, communicate as a warrior on the path of no words; the choice alone was enough. What had he said? "It is only in this choosing that we travel forward on the road to Tunkashila."

It was very quiet as we glided through the water. I gazed up at the moon, more alive to me now, more a part of my life. We had gone quite a way, perhaps half a mile or so. I wasn't tired or cold. We were about a quarter of a mile from the center. As we swam, I was reminded of the sixties when we would go skinny-dipping and sleep out under the stars. The world, everywhere and anywhere, was our playground.

We approached what looked to be the center. Even though the shore seemed very far away, fear was not with me. I felt it out there though, but somehow safe from its clutches.

Black Hawk stopped, treaded water lightly, popping his shoulders emerging above the surface. I did the same.

"We are here, John." I nodded.

"You must remember this place, for we shall come here again," he said.

For no reason a part of me relaxed inside, a part that I had never felt tense. I sighed and closed my eyes for a moment, just feeling the soft caress of the water against my skin. I scooped up a handful and let it run between my fingers. Black Hawk told me it gave life, that it was the blood of life. I saw how that was true and that water was like a little child, precious, needing to be cared for and nurtured.

"John, look from where we came." I did. "Do you see from here that change is possible?"

What did he mean? A deep frown began to set on my face, and a judgment of myself snuck up. I thought quickly, Nope, I won't do that to myself. I just didn't understand, and that was okay. I didn't have to know everything.

For no apparent reason, I became uncomfortable, fidgety, tense. I swam in a tight circle, trying to relax and get back to the good feeling, but I had no luck. I had an urge to dive under. Black Hawk, a few feet away, was looking somewhat curiously at me – the same expression I had seen when I had made the first offering. I still couldn't interpret the meaning. Then, on a sudden impulse, I dove under, kicking my feet up behind me.

I swam down a couple strokes. The deeper I got, the colder the water. My skin seemed to wake up with the cold. When I was ten feet from the surface, I halted my descent and swam laterally. I opened my eyes.

It was dark, but with the moonlight glowing through the surface, not pitch black. I began to feel lonely, sad really. I stopped moving and peered around. Shadows and shafts of light moved in and out of my vision. I couldn't see Black Hawk's feet nor had I any idea where he was. I didn't give the amount of breath left much thought. I just knew I was okay. I let out a laugh at my hanging there underwater with my arms dangling in front of me in the darkness in the middle of a lake. I looked under me and had an urge to swim further down. It was almost a physical pull to dive down. Then, without further thought, I pointed my head down, pulled my arms, and descended. I felt free, like a fish with an endless world to explore. My ears popped at the new depth. This shook me a little, but I kept plunging down. The water grew colder and darker with each stroke. Soon nothing but dense blackness, then nothingness.

The lake began to close in on me. I started to gasp for breath. I stopped, and vaulted myself toward the surface. I looked up to see how deep I was. I saw nothing but blackness. I kicked and pulled my arms harder. My lungs were bursting. Then like a slow bolt of lightning, a thought went through me: I might not make it. It set off a chain reaction of nightmarish thoughts: I was going to die – there was no way out – there were no answers for this wasn't a question – no one could help me, even if they wanted to – there were no decisions to make here – there were no choices – I had no chance to choose – no hope.

My lungs exploding, I flailed my arms wildly, clawing toward the surface. Then suddenly, I just stopped and hung there. A couple of seconds passed. In front of me, I saw a shaft of light. My eyes followed it up. The surface was no more than arm's length over me! I slowly reached up and broke the surface with my hand and pulled the rest of my body easily out into the air.

I wasn't even out of breath. I marveled at the weirdness of all this. One minute I'm drowning, and the next I'm taking a leisurely swim underwater. My eyes focused. Black Hawk was in front of me, smiling.

"Could you see from down there that change is possible?

Was he teasing or asking a serious question?

I looked hard at him and suddenly felt very sad, almost at the point of tears. A feeling was trying to come out of me, but it couldn't tear itself free. Then I remembered that I had felt the sadness when I was underwater. I tried to shake it, but it stayed on top of me.

Black Hawk whispered across the water, his words running, gliding at me over the surface. "John, remember what we have spoken of here. Soon, all will be shown to you."

I nodded. We began to swim back.

We reached shore quickly, pulled ourselves out into the cold air, and dressed. Looking back over the water to where we had swum, it seemed a long way. I glanced over at him, and he turned to meet my eyes. An unspoken message passed between us. I held out my hand, and he handed me the pouch.

I took out a small handful of tobacco and spoke out. My words were loud and seemed to travel over the lake to the opposite bank. "Spirit of the water, thank you for giving us strength. Thank you for giving us life. Thank you, spirit of the water, for letting us have the courage to see that you are truly the source of all life. Help us to have the courage and strength to protect you. I offer this to you in thanks. It is small as compared to all that you have given, but it is given with all our love. A Ho."

I laid the tiny leaves of tobacco gently on the surface, then raised my hand in farewell and honor to the lake where I sensed an important lesson had been learned, even though it had not revealed itself to me. I wondered if life was like that, full of lessons which were not immediately apparent to us especially if we fooled ourselves into believing they were problems, hardships, unfairnesses? Perhaps, I thought, if we give of ourselves, if we honor the earth by trusting, it will, in return, reveal secrets to us and teach us of ourselves.

Black Hawk had stood by my side during my offering and his friendship deepened with his silence. I felt how two people standing together, one in silence, the other speaking his heart, represented all the world needed. It represented all I ever wanted from my fellow man – to be understood without exchanged words, the world inside me to be understood, for that's where I felt the most lonely, the most trapped.

We headed back to the circle. Along the way, I shook my head in awe, thinking how much I had changed in one day, and I was so grateful, humbled by it. The power of change was awesome. Did I mean our power to change, I questioned? I felt close to seeing something. Why did his use of the word "see" baffle me? Why did I have a instinct it was important? Where was the bridge to cross over to find its meaning? I dropped my examination and turned my attention to the surroundings and to walking softly. I had begun to know; we did walk on the blood and bones of our ancestors.

Chapter Eleven

We sat cross-legged on opposite sides of the glowing embers of the fire, me in the north and Black Hawk in the west. A minute of silence passed, then he began.

"John, we have come far on our journey today. It is good."

There was a finality in the way he spoke. A chill went through me. I kept quiet and listened.

"As this has been a journey of spirit for you, it has become one for me. It is so. The light of this knowing was dim. My heart can feel my people, the Sioux, crying in this time. This, John, I must search out."

In an action I'd come to recognize, he took a introspective moment. Perhaps he listened for guidance. Then he spoke again, slowly illustrating each phrase with artful hands.

"Hear me now, John, for I am Black Hawk Who Walks the Wind of the Sioux Nation. We are warriors as one, brothers. You have brought much honor to your spirit."

Pride surged in me.

"You have given of yourself to the spirit of the deer and

the water, and to the ancient Rock People, and to the Great Grandfather Tree, and to our relative, the wind. You walk softly upon our Mother Earth. It is so. A Ho.

"Now I must make the journey to my people, for I have seen that is where my path of spirit lies. I cannot turn my back. My heart, John, feels this journey is filled with many choices and my spirit must be strong, must be open. I will call to my relatives, the wind and the hawk, for courage and strength. I will pray to Tunkashila for guidance. For I will travel the wind to a place far from here, and search out the tears of my people. Ho."

Then he held himself nobly and gazed out at the night. It occurred to me he had been trying to tell me something. I thought about his words. He felt that his people, the Sioux, were crying and that he must search them out. And I had acted as a warrior. But he spoke of making the journey alone…alone. Then it hit me. I turned to him, my chin raised proudly, and my eyes, fierce now, locked with his. The bridge between stood strong. I brought my two index fingers slowly together in front of me, then pushed my palms forward.

He reached across to me. I grasped his forearm as he did mine. We would go together. I saw not only that choices needed to be made but that they needed to be seen. Friendship was on the path of spirit and of great value and worth. I thought, wasn't that what we stood for in the sixties as we marched side by side? JFK, King, Bobby – what was important to them? Hope and Unity. Some say hope died with them. I, for one, hope not.

Chapter Twelve

Black Hawk began again. "The hawk is my spirit animal, my brother. Each one of us has a spirit brother of the four-legged, or the winged, or the fish. It is with his guidance, and that of our brother the spirit wind, that I can journey into the future. How this is possible, I do not know. For some of Tunkashila's work must not be questioned, only listened to and followed. My heart speaks, and Tunkashila tells me to journey now, in this time, to Dakota. John, for you to journey with me, you must call out to your spirit animal."

"How do I know what it is?"

"Do you remember," he started to say with a bit of mischief, "that to see what is in front of you on the path, you must open your eyes?"

"Yes, I have a vague recollection of hearing something about that."

"It is so." He laughed. "All is possible if we open our eyes and look."

I studied the ground and pondered his words, then felt a tap on my head.

"Words, John!"

"Oh, no!" I said, holding my head in frustration. "Okay, I promise I'll never do it again!"

"Walk same path for many seasons and then take new path; it takes time for old way to fade." He smiled.

I nodded, feeling better. We stayed silent for a moment, quieting ourselves. The night sounds seemed also to hush.

Black Hawk began again. "If our eyes are closed to the miracles Tunkashila gives us, then we will not see those miracles, will we?"

I shook my head and told myself: Listen with spirit, John, listen with a feeling. Maybe I was trying too hard.

"It is in the opening that all will be seen. To see the song of the tree, of the river, to hear the heartbeat of the earth. Remember this, and you will prepare the way for the spirits to speak."

Spirits to speak! This made me nervous.

"You have gathered much power today," Black Hawk stated. "For the journey we will make together, much will be needed. Have faith in what I say. Our spirit gathers strength and power only in our acts as warriors and in our choosing as you have done today.

"Listen inside for guidance; ask for guidance. To open is to ask." He interlocked his fingers to illustrate this.

Again, I nodded. I was a little afraid. The meeting of my spirit animal sounded dangerous, overpowering.

"Stay in your heart," he added. "Bring quiet to your

mind. Remember how this is done cannot be spoken of or done with words, only by opening. Do you see?"

I shook my head.

"Let the feeling of spirit come into your body; open your heart. You will see, John. It can only be seen in the doing."

"Okay," I responded. All I could do now was have faith.

"Like the offerings we have made, you must make offering to your spirit animal. We do this with dance."

Dance! That sounded embarrassing. Then I was reminded of the sixties and of how we danced and sang anywhere and everywhere for the pure enjoyment and freedom of it. We were never concerned with what people thought.

Black Hawk continued. "This song was given to me by my grandfather. I offer it to you. Follow your heart, John. Spirit never loses its way. Stay within the Sacred Hoop, for it protects us. We have prepared the way. It is so."

He began to sing a chant of four different phrases over and over again. His voice focused my attention, then the singing pierced through that closed door to the serenity inside me. I shut my eyes and suddenly I was pulled inside myself, in through the door. I began to sway to the beat of his chant. I kept going deeper and deeper and felt as though I were creating a cocoon around me, layering me further from the outside world, from my present environment.

I heard again his words, "open and ask," and saw in a quick visual flash those interlocked fingers. I heard myself call out from the cocoon, "Spirit animal, I call to you and ask you to join with me, my brother."

Within seconds my breathing had altered. It became

deeper, involving my whole body. Never had I breathed this way before. I wanted to pull away from whatever was happening to me, but I stayed with it, I think as a result of the experiences I had had during the day when fear reached for me.

Then, I felt my face changing! My face was being pulled out into another shape! My chin stretched out, longer. My mouth came in close to my chest, and my ears felt as if they were growing larger, narrower. Could this really be happening? If I looked in a mirror, would I see something changing?

Without my conscious command, my head and neck turned to the left in a way that was totally unfamiliar to me. It was without a doubt not a human turn. Even though my eyes were still closed, I felt them widen and peer out searching for something. It was if they had a mind of their own. The wall of fright was right there next to me. I sensed I could release it, and it would slam full force into me. Another choice.

Again, involuntarily, my head turned slowly to the right and set itself at an odd angle. It was then that I knew an animal had come into me. But what kind of animal? The way in which my neck had turned reminded me of something.

I heard Black Hawk's singing grow louder and stronger. I sensed it was a signal of some sort. I quickly understood, and without any hesitation I knew that, to become fully one with this animal, I had to honor and pay homage to it. I stood up and began to dance.

I danced with my eyes still closed in a small tight circle to the beat of Black Hawk's chanting. I picked up one foot and stamped hard into the ground, then shuffled forward, and repeated the step. I held my arms straight out, palms down, and glided them through the air creating circles. I almost twirled. I was lost inside the dance. It was like Woodstock, where we gave ourselves over to the music and the feelings it evoked.

My commitment and passion mounted as I danced. I felt each step I took. Each time my arms glided through the air, I gave myself to my spirit brother.

Silently, I called out, "Spirit animal, my brother, I offer this dance in honor of you and ask that you become one with my spirit."

Almost immediately, my shoulders hunched over and my body started to take a new shape, moving closer to the ground. Suddenly, the identity of my spirit brother of the four-legged was clear to me! It all made sense to me. The day made sense to me. Black Hawk was right, if I had only opened my eyes, I'd have seen it. My spirit animal was the deer.

The deer welcomed me without words. I felt his heart join with mine; we were one. Like the natural facts I was becoming aware of, I knew he was my brother and would protect and guide me.

I had an urge to drop down on all fours, and for a moment this scared me. But I let my fear stay by the side and fell to my hands and knees. I felt my limbs become his. I knew without a doubt that I was the deer in that moment, and he was me. If you had looked at me, would you have seen a deer? I don't know.

My head rose up, and my nose flared out, sniffing the

air. Then my head ducked down and brushed against my forearm or foreleg. I felt fur, not skin. The top of my head felt heavy. Something seemed to be coming from my scalp, but I was too petrified to investigate with my hand.

My head lifted quickly and my ears pricked up to listen. From far away, Black Hawk's song grew louder. I sensed it was time to return.

I called out in the cocoon, "Great Deer, you have honored me. We are brothers of spirit. Thank you for your guidance to this place, and for all that I have learned this day."

I felt him slowly leave my body, which seemed to reshape itself into my human form. I sat up, still within the cocoon, but something had changed. I sensed the deer next to me. He stood by my side as if in vigilance. He had enormous antlers. I counted twelve points. That was what I had felt on my head! Still with my eyes closed, I looked into the buck's eyes and felt the eyes of a warrior. I raised my hand, fingers wide and greeted him, "A Ho." He raised his head in response. He had such dignity and calm; never had I seen such a sureness.

Now I knew I must fully leave the cocoon, so I paced my breathing, slowing it, deepening it. After a moment, I gently opened my eyes and found Black Hawk in the same place, his chant little more than a whisper. I glanced to my right. The deer stood there. He wasn't there in flesh and blood, but some other sense in me could see him.

Black Hawk slowed his chant until he gradually stopped, then looked directly at me and asked kindly, "Are you okay, John?"

"Yes," I said, smiling. I was grateful for those kind words. The meeting of my spirit animal had left me out of balance and somewhat overwhelmed.

"Let us rest till the sun reaches us," Black Hawk said.

I nodded and stretched out on the ground, as did Black Hawk, and fell immediately asleep.

Chapter Thirteen

I woke up to the crackling of the fire. Black Hawk had assembled a spit over the flames and was cooking a rabbit. Edges of light skirted over the trees. Dawn was close.

I sat up and rubbed the sleep out of my eyes. My dreams had been positive, a change from the usual negative scenarios. It was a little cold. The heat from the fire felt good, so I edged closer. Black Hawk squatted flat-footed across from me. I had seen him lower himself into that position so often and had tried to imitate him, but when I attempted to flatten my feet against the ground, I fell on my ass. I was extremely jealous of its contemplative appearance. I suppose I liked the image of the ponderer! Certainly what I had attempted to emulate on the green in Woodstock.

The rabbit smelled good. Black Hawk and I exchanged a smile. The familiar woods were beginning to take on shape and color with the dawn light. A faint mist covered the ground, and the quiet seemed tangible.

I studied the cooking rabbit. "Black Hawk, should we make an offering to the rabbit?" I asked.

Pride and surprise shone in his eyes.

"John, it has been done. Our relative has given himself to us so that we may feed the body. His spirit is strong, and his track, long. May his heart reach to Tunkashila and be blessed."

"A Ho," I responded.

Each moment, even the moment of waking up, was filled with acts of respect and honor – small acts, but I had begun to see and cherish them. An excitement ignited deep within me. I thought, if this is what life has to offer, oh how glorious it could be.

The rabbit was done, and we ate slowly. My eating was not the usual mindless act. I felt my body and spirit fill with the strength of the rabbit's giving and the preciousness of it. Black Hawk had spoken of the circle of life. I began to feel his meaning, to see we were all connected: earth, animal, water, sky, plants, trees. I thought, it's simple, isn't it? Unless we started to be aware, the path of the circle would run into nothing. But for me the simplest of things have been the most difficult to comprehend and accept.

The sun began to edge its way over the trees. We raised our faces to meet it. After a moment, Black Hawk called to me. "John, it is time."

With those words, some part of me deep inside started to panic. My breathing increased and I shuddered slightly. The unknown felt close, and I feared it. What was ahead or what exactly we were going to do, was still not clear to me. I had sudden, flash-like thoughts of backing out. To travel the wind to South Dakota sounded far-fetched. He called this dreaming. Now, faced with it, I didn't think I could really accept that such a thing was possible. I scrambled in my mind for a way out. Then I thought, what am I afraid of? Maybe I knew that if this were possible, then all was possible. Black Hawk had said that we had seen we had a power over ourselves, but that we were scared of that power and its responsibilities.

Black Hawk began to put out the fire.

Transporting ourselves in some supernatural way to South Dakota was beyond all reasonableness and beyond the extraordinary event of finding my spirit brother, the deer, and the philosophy of life he was teaching me. I wondered if this was why we resisted believing in the supernatural? Because if the supernatural proved to be natural, then our responsibility to ourselves, to others, and to our world, would have to change.

It's as if one said, "God, I'll believe in You if You throw down a lighting bolt," and then a bolt cracked down from the heavens. But then one asked Him again, and again another bolt flashed down. One would have to believe then, wouldn't one?

He had finished putting out the fire and was rechecking the dead coals. I pictured myself thanking him as sincerely as possible, and bidding him goodbye, then walking back the way we had come, finding the road, and ending up back in town.

Blackness seem to settle around my spirit. I felt its light begin to flicker out. Where was I, I thought? Why was I really here? Was there really a way to solve my misery? Why am I so miserable?

Thoughts swooped down on me and clouded my mind with their logic. Asking seemed to be a way of life for me, a pulse that never stopped beating. Without questions I felt lost, drowning in the sea of the unknown. Questions and control were my creed and my place to breathe clearly, without interruption from a world which had only faith to call its banner.

I spun out of control on this internal dialogue. I sensed Black Hawk was aware of my dilemma, and he waited patiently for me to find the end of it. There was an end, I thought. I had known this from the beginning of my unhappiness – a life of not doing what I wanted and of not being who I wanted to be. I knew I wouldn't be stuck in this place forever. There was a way out, wasn't there? The possibility that I would remain in this limbo until the end of my life was never even considered.

But so many years had passed, hadn't they? I was still here and still stuck. Did people live whole lifetimes thinking sooner or later their lives would change? Did they keep believing that, right up to their last breaths? Why did that happen? Would it happen to me?

The strength needed to overcome my fear of change seemed insurmountable. I couldn't do it. My eyes searched around the circle for something to help me, to save me, to give me the pill that would make all the searching stop. Why couldn't I just live a normal life? What was a normal life anyway? A life without wanting and needing, a life without the persistent gnawing of "it's greener over the hill."

But how could I run from this chance? I knew I could

because I had been running from chances all my life. I had just never seen them before. They had been there, though. Chances are like flowers; they only grow when they're cared for, watched over, and truly wished for. That was the difference, I thought. I had played at wanting a chance to change my life, but I had never really prayed for one, prayed for the courage to change. I felt defeat come deep into my bones. I knew I didn't have what it took to live the way of spirit, the way of no questions, the way of faith. I turned to Black Hawk to tell him rationally why it was impossible to go with him. I turned and saw him as I always did, as someone I so wished to be like. Still it didn't remove my cowardice.

"Black Hawk, listen." He turned to me. "I want to thank you for everything. Thanks seem not enough, really –" I stopped myself. That's right, they didn't. Why was I running away? How could I turn my back on him now? Maybe he needed me. Maybe spirit needed me. Maybe I needed me…yes, so desperately. I needed the real me to come out, to stay out. I needed to help and touch people. I was so tired of feeling not right inside myself and with the world. Where were the thoughts of courageous deeds and love-filled acts? That was what I wanted to look back on when I faced God. But where did the courage come from to cross over the invisible line and shake the foundations and frames I spent a lifetime building? How could I find the courage to accept my power to change. I could pray, couldn't I? I could pray with all my heart.

I shook my head at him, indicating I had nothing more

to say, and withdrew into the small feeling of spirit that remained. I cried out inside to God. "Please help me, please help me to have the courage to believe that all is possible. Help me to find the courage inside to change, to face the unknown without questions. Help me, Tunkashila, to walk as warrior, with love always in my heart, for myself and for others. God, please, show me how I can help those who need help. I want to feel the rightness of the world and live a life of spirit and love. Tunkashila, I ask this of you and pray to you with everything I am. Help me, God."

Tears ran down my cheeks. I went to wipe them away, and Black Hawk held my hand back. I turned to him to find that fierce pride in his eyes.

"You honor Tunkashila with your asking," he said.

I nodded, not having the words of gratitude for his recognition.

I wanted the chance. I faced him, and my eyes must have shone with it. He raised his hand straight over his head, fingers spread wide, and, as if it were a signal, a warm powerful wind began to blow over us. It swept through the trees causing the rustling sound I loved so much. I listened. My heart gentled. A simple smile formed on my face. I felt very light, soft, like a little boy with innocence in his eyes. I peered around gently, humbly. Everything around me – the trees, the earth and the sky – came to me not as objects, only as feelings. The tall pine tree as dignity, a warrior wanting to protect me with the understanding of a father's touch; the earth under me only wanting to give all of herself to me, only wanting to make sure I was cared for: this was spirit. I could see spirit in all things. I could see how everything and all things were only feelings of love touching us. I could see feelings.

Black Hawk's eyes, like mine, were aglow with the softness of images that seemed to float around us. How could I have asked him to explain the unexplainable? Innocence. What could be more valuable than this understanding, because with it came the secret that all was possible. It was with this knowing that I could believe, riding the wind and traveling to distant places with just a thought and intention was possible. It was time, and I waited for us to come to the threshold of the impossible and create possibility.

Suddenly we heard a loud bird-whistle pierce through the sound of the wind, the same whistle that had led us into the woods yesterday, a hundred years ago. Black Hawk looked up to the sky. The bird called again, "Peeeeee." It was much closer now, somewhere to my right, the sound ominous. Then I saw a black hawk come over the trees. His wings were spread wide, and he floated silently, gracefully toward us. I glanced at Black Hawk for some indication of what to do. He sat rigid, waiting, staring out at the night, no longer watching the hawk's descent. I connected into his feeling and felt a focused edge of power come into my soul. I felt my face darken, my eyes narrow, my back straighten. Peripherally, I saw the hawk fly three feet above the ground toward us. He approached very fast, but as if in slow motion. I knew not to move. He got within ten feet of us, pulled up and landed all in one movement.

The hawk peered directly at Black Hawk, who had still

to look at him. Then the hawk let out a piercing shriek: "PEEEEEE." Black Hawk turned to him, raised his hand in silent greeting, and their eyes locked. Time stopped. I felt I was witnessing an ancient ritual. Black Hawk rose and began to dance with such grace and awareness of movement that it mesmerized me. He converged with the invisible energy and rhythms surrounding him. How could we, as human beings, lose sight of our ability to act in this type of accordance with nature?

The hawk watched him, holding that noble hooked beak high. Its eyes were slits. They were the eyes of Black Hawk when we had pulled the hunters from our relative, the deer. If I had only seen from the beginning, I mused.

Black Hawk danced on as the rising sun came over the treetops. My brother, the deer, waited inside of me. I only had to call out and he would come. I looked to the sky, raised my hands to Tunkashila and said a silent prayer. "Come to me, my brother. Let us travel together to the west, to the place of the ancestors, to the place of the Sacred Earth. Join with me and let us stand as warriors together." Where did such words come from, I wondered. They frightened me. I knew nothing of these things. The sadness began to envelop me again, but within seconds my attention was caught by the buck walking with sureness out of the woods. He embodied a completeness of soul.

I stood and, like my brother Black Hawk, began to dance. I danced with an intention and a commitment of giving something back to those who honored us, to the sacred connection in all things. We danced, Black Hawk in the west quarter of the Sacred Hoop, I in the north. I began to feel light-headed, almost if I were floating. My eyes closed naturally, but my feet continued to find sure steps. I could still see Black Hawk and our brothers, the hawk and deer. Suddenly we shot away from the Hoop. I was in the deer's body, and Black Hawk was the hawk. We flew through the woods, trees rushing by, then skimmed the lake to its center. I followed the hawk as he dove into the water. It was the way I had gone the night before. Black Hawk had said to remember this place.

We plunged through the depths of the water and went through the bottom of the lake and came into a place of sheer whiteness and nothing more. I felt lost. This was a place that required a way of moving that was foreign to me. But the hawk turned and saw my dilemma, and his eyes reassured me that he would guide the way. His wings were spread wide, and he moved laterally without a motion in his wings. I followed his example and, still in the deer's body, lay on my side and glided along through the whiteness. What was this place? A place of transition, perhaps. We came quickly through it as we had through the woods and lake. Then, as if descending from clouds, I saw a forest below. We glided down between the trees, and I suddenly was standing on the ground.

The hawk hovered a few feet over me. He began to fly slowly to the right. I followed on deer's hooves. We moved through the trees. After a quarter of a mile we came to a small well-worn log cabin. It had a familiar look. The hawk flew in through the open doorway. I approached cautiously. I sensed something ominous in the cabin, something I wasn't sure I wanted to see. My deer eyes peered through the front door, and found Black Hawk and myself, in our human forms, sitting cross-legged in a corner of the cabin. They seemed to be expecting us. I followed the hawk to the center of the room. We gazed across at our human forms. Then, without moving, I found myself running through the woods side by side with my human form. Or was I the human form running with the deer? I seemed to be in two places at once. The hawk and Black Hawk were to my left. Black Hawk's face reflected my single mindedness and determination.

Our running through the forest was like the running from the hunters, free and without outside thought.

I was in another world, but where it existed was unknown to me. Was I in a trance of sorts and imagining all this? I didn't think so. It seemed all very real. These were all places which felt familiar and which in some way revealed themselves moment to moment.

Our transition through the woods was quick, as all transitions seemed to be. It shattered my perception of time and distance. We broke into a clearing. There, a beautiful waterfall cascaded fifteen feet into a small pool. We stopped in front of the pool – Black Hawk, the hawk, myself, and the buck. Black Hawk sat down cross-legged on the grass, and I followed. I saw that he was offering a prayer to the falls; I did the same. I wasn't sure what was next, but I didn't feel lost or apprehensive, only excited at the adventure I was experiencing. All fear had vanished.

We finished our prayers. Black Hawk rose and dove into the pool. I followed. The deer and hawk watched from the bank. We swam toward the waterfall. Black Hawk, a few feet in front of me, swam around the charging water and disappeared. When I got to the side of the fall, I saw that he was waiting for me in a small cave directly behind the fall. I climbed out of the water and joined him. Through the clear torrent of water, we could see our spirit animals on the bank. From the expression of seriousness on Black Hawk's face, I knew we were at the final place of transition. He raised his two index fingers to his eyes in the gesture that had begun to mean so much to us, then pushed his palm forward. I raised my two fingers to my eyes and moved them toward him. He stepped forward and dove through the falls into the pool, and I dove after him. We shot like rockets through the water and into the earth at the bottom of the pool. The earth felt like a mother as we moved through her. She comforted and supported me. It was as if I were passing through a mother's womb. It was a remembered feeling.

We broke through into the sky above a land of wide-open space. How we arrived at the ground from the sky escaped me, but we were suddenly standing near a paved road, a highway. The terrain was the flat in all directions, not a building in sight. Was this South Dakota? Black Hawk stared at the road as if its existence was beyond his comprehension. Out of nowhere, an enormous tractor trailer roared by us. Its force buffeted us back a couple of steps. This bewildered Black Hawk. He stood stock still and peered around as if making sure we had landed in the right spot.

Strangely enough, I had accepted the phenomenon of being where we were; it might well be South Dakota. We hadn't spoken a word yet, and I wondered if speaking was possible in this "dreaming state," or even if we were still in it? Everything now appeared quite real, unlike the supernatural transition places we had passed through. Like Black Hawk, I didn't know how traveling to other places and times was achieved.

Black Hawk's eyes followed the two-lane road, split by its yellow line, to the horizon where the truck had diminished to a speck. I spoke up.

"Black Hawk, are you okay?" Speech, then, was possible.

"John," Black Hawk said, "this is the land of my ancestors and their ancestors. What is this that has harmed the Sacred Earth?" He pointed to the road. I didn't know what to say.

He turned around and became even more bewildered by what he saw next – a waist-high barbed-wire fence that stretched in both directions as far as the eye could see. He walked over to it and gingerly touched a pointed barb. Then he silently questioned me.

This confused me. Perhaps the confrontation of elements, such as the fence and road on his sacred land, brought about this reaction.

"It's a fence," I said. His question persisted. "They put it there to keep people and animals off the land. It's farmland. They grow corn, wheat, soybean."

He studied the tilled soil all the way to the horizon,

then walked across the road, gazing sadly at the pavement. On the other side, he found another barbed-wire fence bordering the fields.

"John," he called, mystified, "the land is the same on this side."

I just nodded. He examined the fence and the barbs closely as if they could tell him their true motive. I sat down on the ground, suddenly a little tired, and watched. I realized from the farmland, highway, and truck, that we were in civilization. The land seemed vast. I breathed easier. God's connection to the earth seemed clearer out here. I felt like a small being.

Black Hawk crossed the road and sat by me.

"John, why do they plant all the land?"

"I guess that now there are many more people to feed." He thought on that for a moment.

"But Tunkashila has given all that is needed. Why take more?"

"Money, I guess. I don't know a lot about what's going on out here. But from what I understand, the smaller farmer is becoming a thing of the past. Only the big farms can survive."

"There needs to be balance," he said, leaving no room for argument. I had a feeling he had hit the nail on the head.

He peered into the distance in both directions, then said with the old certainty, "We are east of the Sacred Hills. My heart speaks that we must journey there."

I nodded. He got up without ceremony, and we started to walk up the road, side by side.

Chapter Fourteen

As we walked west, several cars and trucks passed us, and the passengers stared at us as if we were madmen. Perhaps it wasn't a common sight to see two people walking along the side of the highway. I had no doubt now: We were in my era, and in South Dakota. The license plates made that clear – good training from when I was a kid on road trips. After about a half-hour, I thought, Why not see if hitchhiking is still alive and well out here in the Midwest.

"Black Hawk, why don't we see if we can get a ride."

He nodded. He seemed to be very far away. I was worried about him. Witnessing progress on his own land seemed to have really thrown him, though I wasn't sure he would refer to it as progress.

I stuck out my thumb, and as I began the ritual walking backward, I suddenly felt free, with no worries. I was just walking along, out in the wide open space, bumming a ride. Very sixties, I laughed to myself.

A couple of drivers passed us without a sideways glance. No problem. You had to put in a little time before that one willing, trusting good Samaritan came along. After a short wait, one slowed behind us. It was a station wagon loaded with the classic family – parents, couple of kids, all looking very friendly. I waved as they pulled over, and yelled to Black Hawk who was still walking up the road, "Hey, we got a ride."

When he turned and started to walk toward me, I heard tires spin in the pebbles of the shoulder. I turned and saw the station wagon burning rubber to get back on the black-top; the mother was frantically rolling up the passenger window.

"What? Hey...What's the matter?" I yelled.

There was no response, only vivid expressions of hatred aimed at me and especially Black Hawk.

"What do you think that was about?" I asked him.

"Much fear in their eyes."

"Fear? It looked like hate to me."

"Fear and hate are the same," he said. I thought on that. He was right. What we fear has an insidious way of becoming what we hate. It's only in our hate that we feel like we have control.

"What do you think they were afraid of?" I asked.

"I do not know. But it was a fear that kept the light from their spirit. This I could see."

"Should we keep looking for a ride?"

"There is good and bad in all things. It is so."

"Okay." I stuck out my thumb.

Only about ten cars passed in the next half hour, and the expressions I saw ranged from curiosity to lack of understanding. What they didn't understand seemed to stem from me. When an Indian family's car passed, I really set to wondering.

Black Hawk strode ahead of me on the grassy shoulder. Every so often I glanced over my back to check on him, and a few times I saw him peer upward, then raise his hand in what seemed a formal greeting. I looked up but didn't see anything.

A brand new pick-up slowed. I waved and put on my best smile. The driver was in his late fifties, wearing a farmer's hat and plaid shirt. He looked like a nice guy. He pulled up alongside.

"How you doing?" I asked through the passenger window.

"Howdy. Where you headin'?" he responded.

"West."

"You with that Indian?" he asked. He had a very obvious attitude in his voice.

"Yeah. Is there a problem?"

"I don't know what you're doing with an Indian 'round these parts, son, but you in the middle of nowhere here. Your car break down?"

"Something like that?" I responded, getting a touch nasty myself.

"Look, I can give you a ride up to the next truck stop."

"Great."

I yelled to Black Hawk, who had stopped about thirty feet up the road. He looked tentative.

"Hey, we got a ride."

"Mister, maybe you didn't hear right," the farmer said.

"I'll give you a ride; wouldn't leave a human being out here in no-man's-land, but forget that Indian. I don't want him stinking up my truck."

I was too shocked to respond. What was going on here, I thought.

"You gettin' in?" he asked.

"What?" I said. His words broke the spell. "No. Thanks anyway."

I walked away in a daze. The farmer yelled something indiscernible, but definitely derogatory at me as he pulled out.

I caught up to Black Hawk, unsure of what to say to him, or to myself, for that matter. I had been confronted with prejudice in the sixties. What were the words? "Long-hair freak," "fag", "dirty animal"? But this felt different. There was a vileness in this guy's voice that came from some deep place. I wondered why there would be prejudice against Indians? Hell, they were here first. We took their country away from them.

Black Hawk caught my eye, silently questioning what happened. All I could do was shake my head in bafflement. I didn't have the heart or the way to tell him. He was right, his people were in trouble. I nursed a hope that these were isolated incidents. We were hitchhiking in the middle of nowhere; perhaps we looked pretty suspicious.

So I kept walking up the road. I heard Black Hawk's footsteps close behind. Trucks, cars passed, but I didn't want to look at the passing faces and see more of this prejudice. After fifteen minutes I heard a car slow behind us. I tensed, immediately on the defensive. I turned and a dark-haired young woman in her twenties pulled her car up.

"You guys need a ride?" she asked, leaning over the shift.

"Ah, yeah, great," I said. Black Hawk was silent, watching the woman closely and listening in that way he had. I jumped in the front, he in the rear. Black Hawk showed a great curiosity about the mechanics of the car.

"Appreciate this," I said.

"Sure. Where you two going?"

"We're heading west."

"Well, I'm going up about forty miles, then heading north. There's a truck stop there I can leave you off at. You can probably get a ride pretty easily there."

"Great."

"I'm Annie."

"John, and this is Black Hawk."

"Nice to meet both of you," she said. She looked in the rear-view mirror to acknowledge Black Hawk, and their gaze held for a long moment. I felt something connect between them.

"Are you from around here?" I asked her.

"About thirty miles that way." She pointed in the direction from where we had come.

"Beautiful country."

"Hang around 'til winter. It gets down to about seventy below wind chill."

"Wow. How d'you survive it?" I asked, and wondered how Black Hawk's people had managed in those conditions over two hundred years ago.

"You get used to it."

"I imagine."

"Are you Sioux?" she asked Black Hawk, with a focused interest and concern. I wondered what it was about.

"Yes," Black Hawk answered, brightening a bit.

At his answer, Annie struggled with something she wanted to say. Her silent struggle looked familiar to me. She reverted to more small talk to cover her discomfort.

"Where you-all from?"

"Back east…New York."

"Really. Do you have relatives out here?" she asked, and again seemed more concerned than just generally interested.

"Yes, many relatives," Black Hawk said. He smiled for the first time since we'd got to South Dakota, and in some way stressed on "relative", indicating Annie. Like the girl in Woodstock, she sensed his silent message, and a deep smile came into her eyes. We chatted back and forth with her. Annie told us that she had lived back east for a few years but couldn't stand to look at the faces of what she referred to as the bigger-and-better-deal people anymore. I laughed, knowing fully what she meant, since I had been one of them. Black Hawk threw a playful smirk in my direction, knowing, too. It was a relief to talk to this friendly woman after the encounters with those other people. It made me grateful for someone's niceness. Black Hawk said that with light there is darkness and that the hard times made the good times more precious. Her friendliness was a small thing, but it made a difference in the moment.

I could see a truck stop about half a mile up the road.

Annie started to get fidgety. I felt again she wanted to tell us something but couldn't get the words out.

She stopped at the edge of the parking lot. When I turned to thank her, I saw her face was very grave. Something stood still in the car for a long moment. It was tangible, like a vibrating energy. She turned so that she looked at both me and Black Hawk, and her blue eyes shone at us with an incredible intensity. Silence. The path of no words. Black Hawk's dark eyes filled with pride. He lifted his hand, fingers wide, in his traditional acknowledgment. The seriousness of emotion with which I had begun to grow familiar rushed through me. She turned to me. I saw the silent allegiance in her eyes. I raised my palm to her, holding it there, not wanting to end this moment. These were the feelings I wanted in my life. Black Hawk and I got out of the car. Our eyes were on hers until she drove away. As we stood on the cement Black Hawk turned to me and spoke these words, "When you walk path of spirit, John, spirit will find you."

Spirit will find you, I thought. Yes.

Chapter Fifteen

We weaved our way through the tractor-trailers in the parking lot, and when we were fifty yards away from the restaurant, I noticed a sudden commotion at the front entrance. A man was being shoved out the door by four men. The man stumbled backward and fell on the ground. They followed, screaming obscenities at him. Before my next breath, Black Hawk had burst toward the fracas, running at full speed. I broke into a run and followed. As Black Hawk and I got within twenty-five yards, one of the attackers picked the man up off the ground and was threatening to hit him. I saw the lone man was an Indian in his early sixties. He was about five-ten, dark-skinned, with a gray ponytail hanging down his back. He was offering no resistance, and I sensed this was a choice he had made. He faced them with an air of dignity.

Before the man could hit the Indian, Black Hawk rushed forward in a burst of incredible speed. He jumped between the men, and with powerful force, pushed one of the attackers on the ground. It looked as if the man almost bounced off the pavement. Before Black Hawk could further his attack, I saw the Indian quickly grab Black Hawk's arm to stop him. A second later I rushed up to Black Hawk. I was ready to pounce on anyone who made a move toward him or the old Indian.

"What the hell's going on here?" I yelled.

Well, it seemed to diffuse things and they stopped in thier tracks. Or, I thought, the odds were a little more even now; they weren't pushing an old man around anymore. They seemed to grasp this as they absorbed the speed and force of Black Hawk's attack and our readiness.

"Are you with these Indians?" one of them asked me.

"Yeah. Is there a problem?" I said, nastily.

The primary instigator had finally gotten off the ground, looking a little dazed.

"The only problem we got here is – we don't want that hedonist bastard eating here."

"What?" I said. I took a step forward. The old Indian lightly touched my arm. He was indicating to retreat – it wasn't worth it. I did so.

He led Black Hawk and me slowly away, almost like children. With each step Black Hawk appeared as if he were going to turn around and attack – if he did, I'd be right there with him. I looked over my shoulder and saw the men had returned into the restaurant.

The Indian led us silently toward a simple well-worn four-door sedan. We stopped at the front of the car. He turned and faced us, his bearing proud. I knew that this was a warrior. He held our eyes straight with his, taking us in, feeling our presence. Then he slowly raised his palm, fingers stretched wide, and spoke these words, "Hau Kola."

At his greeting the sadness was on me again, but much stronger now. "Hau Kola" reminded me of something, but I just couldn't remember what.

Black Hawk faced him with the stance of a warrior offering his respect to an elder, raised his hand, and said, "Hau Kola."

I snapped away from the pull of the sadness, raised my hand, and said, "A Ho."

We stood tall together as the wind blew across the flat prairie surrounding us. I knew with sureness that this was the beginning of many such silent moments with these two warriors.

"I am Spotted Eagle," the old Indian said.

"I'm John."

"I am called Black Hawk."

We all smiled at one another.

"West of here, there is a good place to eat," Spotted Eagle said matter-of-factly. I wasn't sure whether or not it was an invitation. And what's this thing about west?

"Do you feel like some company?" was the best I came up with to bridge the awkwardness. They exchanged a small mischievous smile at my words.

"What?" I leveled at them.

They broke up, laughing. I at least thought that once we got to South Dakota, all this damn laughing would cease and desist. Little did I know that South Dakota was the home and center of the universe of what they called "joking" each other. I better start getting on my toes or be left in the dust. Later on, Spotted Eagle would explain to me the joking was intentional; it kept us from taking ourselves so seriously and reminded us we were not perfect.

Black Hawk and Spotted Eagle, still laughing their heads off, got in the car.

"What?! Tell me. Come on, I can take it."

This set them into further hysterics.

Within the first minute I'd already been relegated to pupil status, and I didn't like this immediate kinship between them one bit.

"Well if that's how you feel about it. I'll walk." I began to stomp up the road.

They pulled up next up to me. I hoped they knew I was kidding. Black Hawk leaned out the window and imitated the attacker perfectly, "You with them In-dians?"

"Yeah, you got a problem with that?"

We all laughed, and I jumped in the back seat.

As we drove onto the highway, I chuckled to myself about my innocent question, "Do you feel like some company?" What had been clear to them from the first moment had finally dawned on me – Tunkashila had destined us to meet Spotted Eagle.

Chapter Sixteen

As we sped along the straight highway, the edges of the world seemed to be on all sides. I studied hillocks that stood alone in the distance, waiting for deer to graze or men on horseback to stop and sight navigation.

We had pulled out on the highway a good half-hour ago, and, other than our conversation in the parking lot, no words had been exchanged among the three of us. I sensed this was intentional, but I didn't know the reason for it. Then Spotted Eagle spoke. His voice had the melodic intonation I had become familiar with in Black Hawk's tone.

"There is good in everyone, John. We are all created by the same hands. You have to take a look at how people were brought up and accept that they can change."

"Are you talking about those racist jerks back at the truck stop?" I asked.

"If I had responded to their fear, I would be letting them become my teacher and be pulling away from my true teacher."

"But what do you do, just keep taking it?" I asked.

"No, you accept that they can change," he reiterated. I was glad he did, as, I'd missed it the first time. So much for my keen listening.

"You make change by being an example," Spotted Eagle added. I sat back in the seat, considering that. I noticed that Black Hawk had listened intently to Spotted Eagle's words but then continued to stare out at the landscape. It was a heavy stare, and I felt there was something out there he was trying desperately to hear. What, I didn't know. But for some reason the look in his eyes reflected a feeling I felt familiar with.

"Spotted Eagle, are you from South Dakota?" I asked.

Yes, I was born here."

"Why is there so much prejudice against Indians here? I don't understand it."

"Many reasons. The farmers and ranchers aren't satisfied with the land they have, and they want more. They look at the Indian land and see all this virgin territory, and say, 'Look at those hedonist bastards; they aren't even using it. They're letting it stay natural. Think of all the corn I could raise, all the money I could be making'."

"But they're farmers; that's what they do," I responded. "They're just trying to create more crops. I mean, I don't know a great deal about this. Does it have something to do with balance?"

"It has more to do with their motives, which are not just to feed and clothe their families, but to make as much money as possible. They want to get ahead, and be better than their neighbor. They treat the land disrespectfully with these intentions. They take and take and give nothing back. We're seeing the effects of these acts all over the world, not just with farmers."

"You mean the problems with the environment?"

"That's right. The chemicals they have put into the earth, water, and air are coming back to us, aren't they? The loss of rain forests they have cut down little by little is starting to show its effects. But few are seeing another change, and that's what they call natural disasters – hurricanes, earthquakes, floods. They aren't natural, but a sign. In the last couple of years we have seen more and more of these signs from Mother Earth. Scientists are now saying that the destructive way we have treated the earth is the reason for these disasters. They try and make it logical, eh? If this logic brings awareness of the abuse – good. But I say this to them – it is a sign of things to come and the beginning of a great change. The earth is changing, John, and it is change that is natural and the way of God."

"What do you mean 'great change'?"

"A great change is coming. Maybe not on our journey, John, or in our lifetime. Change is the way of God. We must listen in our hearts, for the signs given by the Grandmothers and Grandfathers. The wind, the rain, the water, the earth are our relatives. They are the Grandparents."

His serene confidence in the prophecy of a great change left me without an immediate response. I felt hopeful, though, at the possibility of great change. I asked him more about the racial problems.

"Spotted Eagle, does their hatred have something to do

with the way they were brought up?"

"Yes. If someone is preaching into your head from the time you are born that this race of people is a bad, terrible people, of course, as you grow older, when someone says they are such and such a race, your first reaction is to destroy them. John, you have to remember, the Indian people are an embarrassment to the government and especially to people who live where reservations are staring them in the face. See, deep down, the government and people in general know what they have done to the Indian is in opposition to all the laws that they say they live by. And instead of doing what is right – admitting their wrongs and then going from there – they turn that shame and fear of one day being called out in the open against us. They turn it into hatred, and with that hate have made destroying us right in their minds. Restitution means nothing if is it forced upon us.

"Even today a war is being fought against the Indian people as it is against other races. Even though it is a silent war, it still takes the lives of my people. There are only a few of us left, John, but those few can make a difference, and this is what scares those in power. My people, who follow the old ways, are feared. Those who live from mind know that spirit is great and can bring change. History has proved this."

"What do you mean 'silent war'?" I asked. I had a feeling that I knew what he meant. But I was to learn much later that the extent of the conspiracy against the Native American Indian was far greater than the wildest stretch of my imagination, frighteningly so.

"Silent war, John, can mean many things, eh? A war can be waged against people by the hatred in other's hearts and eyes or it can be waged, hidden, behind closed doors. If it were to show itself, it would reveal the wrongs, injustices, and shame of its intentions. It is in this silence that a war is being fought against the Indian people--a war behind a closed door."

He hesitated and, I think, listened inside for guidance.

"I feel in my heart, John, it is not the time to talk a great deal about the silent war. There is another path to walk before you can truly see without judgment the war against my people and others. When it is time, the path will reveal itself. I say this to you, though, there are books written about these injustices. I hope in my heart that people will pay attention to them; they are written by warriors. It is like all things, the spirit will come if we truly want to know."

(It was upon his words that later on I discovered the books and the extent of the "silent war." I decided upon Spotted Eagle's and Black Hawk's agreement not to illustrate fully or in detail that conspiracy. Others had spent lifetimes gathering and living the information. Subsequently, they are more qualified than I to tell that story; they are true warriors. And perhaps I cannot speak now, in this time and place, without judgment or in a way that those acts of war need to be spoken about.)

"There are only one million four hundred thousand Indians left," Spotted Eagle said. "But as I said, there are still those who walk the path of spirit and see the future. Ho."

"What has happened to my brothers and sisters who

have fallen from the path?" Black Hawk asked Spotted Eagle.

"The fire of their spirit has been buried by the many lies that have tested us, my brother."

"Does not the Earth, our Mother, keep their spirit full?" Black Hawk asked.

"We started with seven hundred thousand acres many years ago, but they have slowly taken a piece at a time away from us, promising us many things. The land is no longer in one piece as it once was, but parceled here and there. They offer us millions of dollars for the land. Even from the time of the colonists they haven't understood why we don't sell the land. How can we sell the land to them if we don't own it? It is the blood and bones of our ancestors."

"It is so," Black Hawk responded. Then surprisingly, he did not inquire any further into those injustices done to his people.

"You know, John, people think they own the land, but they never will," Spotted Eagle said. "The land owns them, because one day they will have to return to that land no matter what they do, no matter how many caskets and vaults they build. They, too, are going to disintegrate and become part of the earth. But they dread that thought because they think the heart of the earth, the ground they walk, is dirty and beneath them. In the old way, we know that we are no better than this land and that when our feet walk upon Mother Earth, we know we are stepping upon many of our relatives. That's why we always talk about walking softly."

I was grateful Black Hawk had taught me this; I absorbed what Spotted Eagle said so much more deeply on hearing it a second time.

"If we were to sell the land, it would be like selling ourselves," Spotted Eagle went on. "It would be to us as prostitution is to them. In our prayers, we thank the Earth for the gifts She gives to support this life, this shell, this spirit. We pray Her children will be many and all will be as it once was so their children can see our Mother as she truly is. But they don't care about the future. If they really care, if they really love their children, why do they persist in letting this world become a wasteland? Why not try to make things better for their children?"

"I agree a hundred percent with you on that," I said.

Spotted Eagle smiled at me in a manner I didn't like. My simple statement had revealed something to him. Black Hawk smiled too. Having no shame in my insecurity, I attacked.

"What's with you guys, can't I speak here?"

"You are not alone in your thoughts, have you sought to know of this?" Black Hawk smiled at me.

"Yes, I remember."

"This is the way."

"I don't get it."

"Must find place of spirit, John, to listen."

Black Hawk had spoken the secret words to shut me up. I sulked back on the seat. It appeared as if I was back to square one. DAMN! I began to plan a way to redeem myself.

We drove for about another fifteen minutes in silence, then pulled off into a truck stop. My body went immediately on the defensive. Black Hawk and Spotted Eagle appeared relaxed and as if looking forward to getting inside. I wondered about this.

We got out and walked through the front door of the restaurant. We were met by the traditional stares toward new customers walking in, but I could see a tenseness around the patrons' eyes that was not traditional. It was subtle, but there, and I sustained my guard. We sat down in a booth and checked out the menus. As we ordered I noticed Black Hawk seemed to be adapting quickly to the mechanics of my era. I watched in awe as he ordered up quite a meal.

Our conversation in the car had sparked a barrage of opinions and information I wanted to illicit from Spotted Eagle. As I planned an approach, I found Black Hawk regarding me with the infamous smile. I gave him my best "okay, tell me" look, and he did.

"All questions must be listened to with spirit and asked with spirit – all questions. Even ones that give shadow that they are about facts, about details. Don't be blind to spirit behind details, John, for that is where the understanding lies, that is where the touch of change lies, not in the listening to details."

I felt defeated. I thought that the desire to hear the details of the problems out here in South Dakota was positive, that it expressed my caring and desire to help.

Spotted Eagle sat quietly and listened. I knew for some reason that his listening was without judgement, without mind. I confronted Black Hawk with my thoughts.

"John, remember, that all change – all change comes from the heart. No matter what your scientists and leaders tell you." His use of the word scientist surprised me. I thought he referred to shrinks.

Black Hawk continued. "To change, to touch others, you must, as Spotted Eagle says, be an example, as he was to us when you and I wished to harm those men. I thank him for his guidance. You will never lead yourself or others with the mind, only with the softness of the cloud-beings in your voice and with the gentlest of the breeze we have felt together in your touch. Only with the love of Mother Earth in your eyes can you open the doors. This knowing has become bright to me again. I thank Tunkashila for touching my spirit. Through our journey the roots of this knowing have grown deeper. Ho. The answers you seek will come to you if you stay on the path. You know of all this, John. It is so."

He was right. I saw how his actions of softness and love had changed me. The questions I held in my mind and heart had been answered naturally by him without my solicitation.

Our food came, and we ate in silence. I studied the other patrons and noticed a marked difference between them and the inhabitants of the East. It was as if these people sat inside their lives; there wasn't a bone in them that was concerned with getting ahead or wishing they were someone else.

I turned back to the table and was met by the steady gaze of Spotted Eagle. It unnerved me, but then my eyes seemed to soften into his, and I relaxed. Everything seemed to go quiet around us. I felt that he was understanding something about me. Then, with two fingers, he drew an imaginary circle in the air in front of him. I watched his hand move slowly around. I felt as if I were in a trance. He completed it; then, like a bubble bursting, the noise and people around came back into focus. It was almost as if it hadn't happened.

What was he trying to communicate to me? I looked to Black Hawk to see if he was aware of Spotted Eagle's action. He was. His face was dead serious. He held my eyes tightly, then raised two fingers and moved them slowly away from his eyes.

I shook my head.

Black Hawk moved one hand laterally like a snake and crossed the other hand over it. I knew he was illustrating the analogy of crossing the river – Do you stop or keep walking?

I smiled. Then gestured with our two-finger sign, and he grinned, happy that I had understood.

I didn't feel in the least awkward communicating in this silent way among other people.

The check came, and I paid it. I was glad I could take care of these warriors in this small way; they had both given me so much already.

As we walked to the car Black Hawk spotted something in a field in front of us and with a big smile, bounded off. Getting to the field he picked several plants gently but purposefully out of the ground, then deposited tobacco in the picked spot. He returned to the car and held up a dozen grayish, brushlike plants, each about nine inches long.

"What is it?" I asked.

"Sage. It is sacred among my people," Black Hawk said.

"What it is used for?"

"Purifying."

"What do you mean?"

"To make us pure and open to the love of Tunkashila we burn the sage and pass the smoke over that which we carry with us on our journey."

"Like what?"

"Like ourselves," Black Hawk indicated. "We bring that which is of the earth into our spirit, into our body. It is in this way that we honor and join with our Mother, and She heals that which is not of spirit. The joining, the accepting, is of importance – only this."

His words sparked the unknown sadness to envelop me again. What was it about, I yelled through my head. It seemed to be coming on more and more frequently.

Then, spontaneously, I said, "Could we, now?"

They both peered closely at me. They seemed proud of me; I thought I saw tears in their eyes. They stood very still, very tall, side by side, in a picture I would always carry with me.

"Yes, John, it is good medicine to burn sage before our journey," Black Hawk said.

Black Hawk pressed together the leaves from two of the sage plants and formed a small rectangular bundle. He lit the bundle, cultivated the growing flame for a moment, then blew it out. It began to smoke. He raised the bundle, bowed his head and offered a prayer to the North. Spotted Eagle lowered his head and pointed in the same direction. I followed Spotted Eagle's lead. After we stood to face in each of the four directions, Black Hawk offered the sage to Tunkashila and Mother Earth. Then, as the sage still smoked, Black Hawk faced Spotted Eagle who waved the smoke in around his face. Black Hawk made the sign of the Sacred Hoop with two of his fingers on Spotted Eagle's forehead and over his heart. Black Hawk repeated the ritual with me, and I, in turn, received the smoke and the blessing. Black Hawk finished by holding the sage up once again to Tunkashila.

I felt the peace I had begun to know since I had teamed up with my friends – Black Hawk, Spotted Eagle, and God.

Chapter Seventeen

"Are we near the place where our brothers and sisters of the Sioux keep their lodges?" Black Hawk asked Spotted Eagle.

"Yes, I think we're near part of one of the reservations," Black Hawk just nodded, affirming that he wanted to go there. Spotted Eagle covertly glanced at me, hinting at a feeling of concern.

The next exit came up, and we got off. We drove another fifteen minutes on an interior road. Then I saw the abandoned farms. It was a wholly sad site. The full impact of what I had read about the small farmers folding up stared me in the face, and I didn't like it. I cursed the government, the whole lot of them.

I considered these farms—America—beyond what Spotted Eagle had told me about the tension between the Indians and the farmers, I knew these hollow structures were not effects of that tension. It wasn't an issue of more land but of price for their products. The sight of these deserted buildings which had been standing perhaps since before this century angered me. I felt that spark, which had begun with Spotted Eagle's talk of the problems with the Indians, grow larger. This was the spark that had led me through the sixties and had set fire to my heart and voice – an angry voice speaking out against what was just plain not right.

"Over there," pointed Spotted Eagle. A hundred yards off the road stood a row of box houses constructed of thin prefabricated material. These houses were tiny, more like shacks.

"My people live in these places?" Black Hawk asked Spotted Eagle.

"Yes. When the government broke another promise about the land, they gave us these houses as an offering. Families of six, sometimes more, live in them."

"The old ones – the grandmothers and grandfathers?" Black Hawk asked.

"Yes, them too. There are Sioux who have worked, who have followed their spirit and have broken out of these places, but they are few."

"Why are the conditions so bad," I asked Spotted Eagle. "I thought the government allocated millions of dollars each year to the Indians?"

"We see very little of that money. It gets eaten up by new jobs the BIA continues to create in their organization or by just plain corruption."

"What's the BIA?"

"Bureau of Indians Affairs," he said. "Indians in this organization fall prey to the power and fortunes offered by the government. Intentions to help their tribes are forgotten. I'm sure this is not unlike the white politicians. The government works on you. But there is the good and the bad, John."

I was surprised when he mirrored the words of Black Hawk, who again didn't show a great deal of interest in what Spotted Eagle had said about the BIA and the moneys involved. I think that, like me, Black Hawk was more concerned with the results.

We drove down the dirt road leading to the houses. No one was around; I thought that strange and asked Spotted Eagle. He just shrugged sadly.

Black Hawk stared out at the tiny houses, an expression of disbelief on his face. It made me want to run and shout my head off at any one who contributed to this injustice. I didn't need to know the hows and whys; it was right in front of me, and real. Something needed to change. This was the proud anger I wanted to carry into battle. Here was the sword I wanted to carry. But, I remembered, this was not the sword of softness Black Hawk had spoken of in the restaurant. It was difficult not to react in anger to these injustices.

"I saw that our people did not walk the earth as they once had, but this I did not see," Black Hawk said. "How is it possible, my brother, that we have come to this place?"

"People don't know what's going on out here; they don't want to know," responded Spotted Eagle. "If they opened themselves to the problems of the Indians, they would have to open themselves to what they hide from – their own spirituality." Black Hawk nodded.

I leaned over the seat and asked Spotted Eagle. "What do you think happens to people? Why are they so scared by their own spirituality?"

"A lot of people live from mind and greed," Spotted Eagle answered. "They don't call it greed though, they call it capitalism, which is about people not really working but striving throughout their life to get ahead. But in their system, there never is 'ahead.' You can never reach that endpoint.

"If you reach out and truly give of yourself, you will have to open your eyes and see how you're leading your life. And some people don't want to look too closely at their lives. This is why they convince themselves that change is not possible. With change, there will be a sense of balance. Everyone will be equal and money will mean nothing. The world will no longer see starving people. But as result of this balance, people will have to give up their servants, give up feeling like a god on a pedestal. They will become equal with people down at the bottom. Where in the white people's way did God say in your life strive to make a lot of money, strive to be ruler over people? This was never mentioned. It was an idea that was created so that people would change their way of thought and feel right in a society where getting ahead is honored."

"But aren't you only talking about the very rich? What about the just the average person?" I asked.

"Yes, that's right. But this kind of thinking filters down to all levels. For each man the battle against what he truly knows is right in his heart is different. People must ask themselves what it is that scares them about being equal with the poor, with other races, with just other people. They must ask themselves why they resist this balance. If they're honest, their answer may be 'Because then, how will I feel good about myself? I will have nobody to feel better than, to feel more superior than. I might have to feel good about who I am on my own. I might have to see and find out that I am truly a good person.'"

"What about the people who are just trying to survive, just trying to get by," I asked.

"Are those people happy?" Spotted Eagle asked.

"That's a hard question to answer. If I had to make a generalization, I'd say, no, they're not.

They're more concerned about surviving, putting food on the table."

"They get caught in a vicious circle, eh? Even though a person knows he's not happy, he continues to turn his back on his true path, whatever that may be."

"But why do they really do that?"

"Fear in having to trust in something they can't see – the future. See, John, if you think from fear, you act from fear. Fear is really a state of mind; it's a choice. But people don't want to believe that. They'll do anything not to believe fear is a choice each of us makes. They'll even give their lives, as many wars have proven. With no fear, there is no war. It's so much easier to not believe that we have control over our own lives. But the funny part is, if you live from your heart, if you live from your spirit, then all that appeared difficult and insurmountable, like leaving the job you hate, or maybe standing up for what you believe, is truly not only easy, but welcome and joyful. Having faith becomes a joyful thing, not the struggle the mind sees. But you must live and see from your true nature to feel these things. With the first step on this path, all that seemed impossible is no longer."

I felt a spark of hope trying to ignite. It no longer had to be a struggle; that sounded good to me. But then I questioned – when you're in the middle of bills, a family to support, and all those other very real things that keep us from doing what we really want to do, you feel trapped. Then, instead of admitting to being trapped, you say "I really have no choice in this. I have bills and responsibilities." Perhaps there is only faith. But to let go and jump off, well…? I wondered if these were the details Black Hawk spoke of?

Part of me wanted to work this out on my own, so I tried to quiet down. I sat back and watched the beautiful landscape of South Dakota. I tried to picture what it must have been like two hundred years ago when telephone poles and fences didn't cross the land. I could almost envision bands of Indians on horseback, traveling across the prairie.

"John, did you see?" Black Hawk asked me.

"What?"

Spotted Eagle pulled over quickly.

"Walk back and you will find a gift from our relative," Black Hawk said.

"Back on the road?" I questioned. He nodded. Spotted

Eagle seemed to know what he was talking about.

"What is it?" I asked.

Black Hawk smiled and said, "A gift."

I got out, jogged back on the side of the highway, and searched for something that would qualify as a gift. I got about a hundred feet when I saw, laying on the grass, a group of six or seven brown striped feathers still intact. I didn't know the species of bird. I hesitated, searching for the best way to pick them up, then just trusted I would be gentle.

Spotted Eagle waved to hurry back.

"I want to leave some tobacco," I yelled back at him.

"The words are enough, John," Spotted Eagle shouted.

As I ran back to the car, I whispered a short prayer, thanking my relative, the bird, for the gift. I jumped in the back, and we pulled off.

"What's the big hurry?" I asked Spotted Eagle.

"I wasn't sure which of the winged had left these feathers and the law tells us that without a permit we cannot have the gifts offered by our relatives, the hawk and eagle."

"Really?"

He nodded. I wondered why, but didn't ask.

I handed the feathers to Black Hawk. "They're beautiful. I don't know how you spotted them."

Black Hawk admired the feathers. "Spirit touched me" – he pointed to his chest – "I looked up and the feathers – " He gestured that they had floated up in the air.

"Really?"

"On our journey there are many relatives of the four-legged, winged, and others who may come to greet us. This is the way when we walk the path. You have seen this."

Black Hawk held the feathers up and said, "Ho Tunkashila."

"Tail of the earth eagle," Spotted Eagle said.

"What's the earth eagle?" I asked him.

"Turkey."

"Oh. I like that."

"For you." Black Hawk offered me the feathers.

I was surprised and took the feathers from him. I did so tentatively, perhaps wondering why I deserved them. I patted them with my fingers and felt their softness. The feeling of spirit came into my heart, and once again the world changed color.

"Thank you," I said.

CHAPTER EIGHTEEN

My love for the land of South Dakota grew with each mile we drove. I knew that corporations and others asked what was so important about preserving the land, and I understood now why people asked such questions. The preciousness of the land and our living connection to it can only be understood through a feeling and never comprehended through logic. A difficult argument to wage battles with. Perhaps the sword of the soft word was the way to make change. I just wasn't sure how to find it or carry it.

Spotted Eagle released me from my thoughts. "Where I live, John, they're many who think my ideas and the way I live is crazy, and, you know, that's okay. My family lives mainly on everyone else's discards. I work with an organization called SHARE that ships used clothing and school supplies to other countries. We're recycling. But nobody wants to do that because it isn't cool to wear someone else's clothing, not unless money says it's okay. Then it becomes a fad, eh? It always comes back to money. Every year the fashion has to change, why is that? If there wasn't fashion, that industry would fold up. The money wouldn't continuously circulate if we all wore... say...blue jeans all the time."

"But what about all the jobs that industry supports?" I asked. "I mean, I agree with you, but it's not that simple. What are the – " I stopped myself. Were these the details Black Hawk spoke of? But damn, in this instance, they seemed important. Odds were Black Hawk was smiling again. I went ahead anyway. "I agree with you, but aren't you oversimplifying, what are the practicalities?"

Spotted Eagle laughed. "John, I'm just talking about encouraging a feeling, eh?"

"This is where I get confused," I said to him. "Between understanding what you're saying and not getting caught in the details. You know what I mean?" I thought this confusion sounded familiar. A mischievous look passed between them.

"John, what do you think?" Spotted Eagle seemed to enjoy asking his question.

"About what?"

"Your question."

"Which one?"

"Good question," he said.

"Okay, what do I think?" They both nodded, looking like Laurel and Hardy. "I think I want to stop and use the facilities."

Spotted Eagle pulled over on the shoulder. Then they

turned back to me, both sporting big proud smiles. I smiled back, jumped out, and was pressed by strong gusts of wind. It felt good out in the open. I had an urge to trek across the endless plain in front of me, feel its history, listen for its secrets. I couldn't get over the vast openness of the country.

I returned to the car, leaned on the window, and said, "Can we stop somewhere and walk around a bit?"

"Soon there will be a place which will speak to you, John," said Black Hawk. "It is not far."

I jumped into the car and we drove on. Even though I was concerned about Black Hawk's continuing silence, he seemed more relaxed since we had met Spotted Eagle and as we drove further west.

"The land speaks strongly out here, John," said Spotted Eagle. "Because we still honor it the way it was meant to be honored. It's a hard life here in South Dakota. Sometimes you can get a wind-chill close to a hundred below."

"A girl who gave us a ride earlier mentioned that."

"The weather can change quick. The next day it might be sixty," he said. "I've seen summers where the wind is blowing thirty miles an hour and it's hundred degrees out. It makes you strong and appreciate everything you have. The changing shows you the way of life."

"Ho Tunkashila." Black Hawk suddenly spoke. I leaned over the front seat and looked a question at him.

"Coyote," Black Hawk said, and pointed to the right.

"Where?"

He pointed again, and I squinted my eyes trying to find it but had no luck.

"I don't see it."

"You look too hard. Let your spirit be open, and the many relatives that walk upon the earth will touch you."

"Okay."

After a couple minutes, when I felt it was safe, I began to scan both sides of the plain. First the feathers, now this. I'd beat them to the punch on the next sighting.

"My brother, your eyes make a big hole in the back of my neck," Black Hawk joked, rubbing his neck.

"What do you mean?" I asked. They laughed. "Okay, okay, but I'm not as good at this as you guys, I was just trying to get a head start."

"The easier way, remember?" Black Hawk smiled.

I nodded and retreated back into the seat. He was right. I wasn't willing to trust my instinct to feel the spirit of the animals and birds. I gave into what I knew, my mind. Perhaps not only with the animals but also with my relatives of the human race.

"You know, John, miracles happen today just as they did one or two thousand years ago," Spotted Eagle said. "I have seen things happen you would not believe. God is alive and well. But even now they're trying to destroy the concept of a higher being, a higher force. People don't want to believe in miracles. It's easier to run to the doctor, or to money, then you don't have to give to yourself. But let's say something did happen, and God did answer their prayers, then they might have to give truly to that belief. But they don't want to, because they want their moral fiber to decay – unknowingly, of course. It's innocence, eh?"

There it was again, I ruminated – innocence.

Spotted Eagle went on. "That decay gives them the right to do anything they want. If they don't like that tree? 'Oh, just chop the damn thing down; we're humans, we have right to do that, we own the land.'

"See, John, as long as we don't have a strong belief in God, or say, just the goodness of man, it gives us an open door to do anything we want. Again, society is structured around this way of living. As Indians, we know we have to abide by that Being, because it is He who has given us life. When I wake up in the morning I say, `Thank you for this day, this life, for food and shelter, and the health of my family. And what will You have me do in this life today to make things better for my children and their children and the children of the future?'"

"Ho," said Black Hawk.

"That's beautiful," I said. "The children of the future. It's frightening to consider what they may have to face."

"If we really love our children, why not try to make things better for them?" Spotted Eagle suggested. "But it isn't by buying more and more clothes or cars or missiles, but by giving them fresh water to drink. Why are there chemicals in the water? Because it costs too much money to clean it up. My grandmother said this to me: `In the time of the great change, people will give all they have for a cool clear glass of water to quench their thirst.' That time is already here. Where do you find clear water to drink? Twenty years ago, no one would've ever dreamed we'd be buying water by the gallon. We had all we wanted in the taps. So, that time is already here. Now, it only costs a minimum, but what will it cost thirty years from now?"

The stark reality of paying for water sunk in with his words. I was thrust back to the place I had experienced in Woodstock, called, "What can the individual, the average man do about the problems with – for example – water?" I had asked myself this type of question many times, but always ran from really trying to answer it. It spoke of my limbo and of the fear of our spirituality that Spotted Eagle referred to. I was tempted to question Spotted Eagle further on my dilemma but feared reprisals from Black Hawk who played the watcher of my instinct. And I began to know the words of my instinct – "You'll never get it by listening with your intellect or from desperation."

"They say history repeats itself," Spotted Eagle continued. "We've seen wars that have killed tens of thousands of men. We should learn from that, not say history repeats itself. To me that's just plain stupid. History is supposed to be a teacher; it gives us the ability to learn from our mistakes. But first you have to admit you made a mistake, and this is one thing the government doesn't want to do – will not do. So they carry on wars without our knowledge. It's the same with people. If you're brought up hearing, 'Johnny, you shouldn't have done that,' of course you'll be afraid to make mistakes, and the first thing you do is relieve yourself of the burden of decision. People are doing this right now with the government – 'Hey I didn't vote for that. They're the bad guys, not us.'"

"People don't feel they can have any affect on those

decisions," I blurted out.

"Is that what you know to be true, John?" confronted Black Hawk.

His gravity stopped me in my tracks. I searched my mind frantically for an answer, a sound rationalization. I quickly became lost in the details of what could be done, what had been done, and why it wouldn't work. Soon my good feelings were gone.

"I don't know," I answered.

I was suddenly depressed. They left me alone, and five minutes later I felt us slowing. I looked up to see a gas station/mini-mart. We pulled up next to a pump and got out. It was strange to see a resemblance of civilization after being on the barren highway.

"I'm going in. Do you two want anything?" I asked.

They shook their heads, and both appeared far away in their thoughts. I sensed that they both thought on the same thing. I didn't know exactly what, only that it might be ahead of us.

"Okay, I'll be right back."

I walked into the mini-mart, and was met by the sight of every imaginable type of junk food. I circled around the racks and found myself a brownie. I paid the young guy behind the cash register, whose simple, unassuming niceness was a surprise to me. I thanked him, wished him a good day, and headed out the door. My mood had changed, and I felt terrific. As with Annie, these brief encounters of pure humanness made me believe in the goodness of man and myself.

As I walked outside, the wind moved across my face. I thought, No matter how hard I try, I will never fully understand my affection for the wind. Perhaps it made me feel I was not alone, that somebody cared, somebody backed me up.

Black Hawk and Spotted Eagle were already in the car. I jumped in the backseat and immediately ripped the paper off my brownie, which produced a loud crinkling sound. They turned around to see what the noise was about.

"Do you guys want a piece?" I asked. They laughed, shaking their heads. We pulled back out on the highway. When I thought they were preoccupied, I bit into the brownie and tried to chew quietly.

"My spirit hear big beaver," Black Hawk announced.

"Yes, very big...big teeth," added Spotted Eagle.

"Very funny," I said.

Chapter Nineteen

"We're all guilty, John," Spotted Eagle said. We had driven about a half an hour in a comfortable silence. I leaned over the front seat to listen.

"I've been in many a restaurant and watched someone order a twenty ounce t-bone, then eat six ounces and slide the rest away. And you know, people joke when that happens and say, 'What about the starving people?' and then everybody laughs. Yeah, what about the starving people, I want to ask them? It's a little thing, John, but in the end it can mean a great deal, not only to your spirit, but to a universal spirit. It's the act itself that has hurt us as a people and buried our spirit, buried change."

"I'm not quite following you. What do you mean, the act?" I inquired. They both cracked up.

"WHAT, WHAT?!" I yelled at them. "Never mind. Okay, okay, I know."

It was hard to believe I still didn't listen appropriately. But these lapses and embarrassments proved valuable later on; I caught myself so much easier. Spotted Eagle gave me another chance.

"What I'm saying is not so much about the details but about the act of going against what you know is right in your heart. This is the act that has hurt us as a people. If it changes, then the details will follow."

"You mean the details of starving people?!"

"Yes, that's right. An injustice as great as that – or maybe something like bad-mouthing the guy who's up for the same job – or, on other side, not standing up for what you know is right in your heart – or, just simply, not following your heart. See, John, it's not only the things we do, but the things we don't do. This is what I was saying about burden of decision. People say they're not part of the system, but the system is made up of individuals whether they voted for it or not. It's still them, because the system says it represents them."

I felt his opinion on the system made sense, but I couldn't see how that sense would help me change the system. Then it occurred to me that perhaps why I couldn't was that I was listening with my mind again. I was listening with my frames of reference and was processing his words through the filters, causing an inability to listen without preconceived conclusions. I did exactly what I accused the system of doing.

"John," Spotted Eagle called to get my attention. He pointed up ahead to a fenced-in area about two hundred yards off the road.

"What is it?"

"Missile silo."

Like the abandoned farms, the results stared me in the face. My reaction surprised me, for it was without words, without anger. Only a cold stillness swept through me, a foreboding.

We pulled onto the shoulder and got out. Cars whizzed by us as we stood side by side and stared across at the silo. It was in a small fenced-in area surrounded by beautiful prairie. There were no buildings, only one blinking red light and a large sliding door leading underground or leading to the sky. I had never imagined it standing amidst this beauty. It made its effects even more devastating.

"Is this the fire that can harm Mother Earth?" Black Hawk asked me. I nodded. He reached over and put his hand on my shoulder. I thought, Here was the final result of man's lack of belief in himself and his innate goodness. I will never forget its silent waiting.

We got back in the car and continued on, lapsing back into silence. I watched the missile silo fade in the distance and reflected a day, months ago, when I sat in front of the television. The screen had suddenly gone to "Emergency Announcement," and I had felt my heart stop. For the briefest of moments I had thought, This is it, and oh, what a waste. How could it be? HOW COULD IT BE? Do you hear me in Washington, in all those countries that have nuclear weapons? How could you do this thing? Why? How could you ever justify this act against humanity? How you could live knowing how possible an accident was? How could you possibly justify it in your hearts – your hearts buried underneath your fears. How could you justify that any existence of such a weapon was right? How could we as human beings let them do it?

Now, as we sped along, I was overwhelmed by that frustration that had kept me cold in Woodstock. But this time, as with the farms and reservations, the frustration turned quickly to an anger I wanted to act on. Couldn't I make change from anger, I deliberated. It felt right and alive and fueled my motivation. How could I give it up? We had felt this motivation in the sixties, though perhaps then, we also had to grow. We who had spoken of tunnel vision and archaic thinking, did we see that the tools, the motivations for the Movement, needed to evolve? Dr. King and Gandhi had seen the possibilities. Would my actions be more enjoyable if I acted from a place of spirit, thus easier and more accessible for others to examine? Perhaps, yes.

Spotted Eagle motioned to Black Hawk to something on the right. Black Hawk gestured for me to look. I looked over and saw nothing. "I don't see anything," I complained.

He pointed up in the sky and parallel to the car.

"I see them!" I shouted. Two hawks circled.

"'Bout time." Spotted Eagle laughed.

"We have passed many relatives since the coyote, John." Black Hawk smiled.

"What?? Why didn't you say something?"

"We didn't want to make you feel bad," Spotted Eagle said. They roared with laughter.

"Thanks, I appreciate it."

Black Hawk faced me with a soft smile on his face and

pressed his palm gently against his chest. A glow came back into my eyes. Listen for the relatives with spirit, open the door inside, he was saying. Here is where they will touch you. I made the two finger gesture away from my eyes and smiled in thanks.

Spotted Eagle started to talk again, and I noticed my listening had changed. It was not his words that were in the forefront of my listening, but the feeling of spirit which came from my eyes and the middle of my chest. It was a soft, centered feeling, relaxing. I listened through there.

"Individual goodness, individual spirit, can bring great change, John. It's Tunkashila, God, who gives us spirit. Which is more powerful, God or mind created by man? History has proven a man or woman who is of great spirit can bring change. Not necessarily the one who has the most convincing facts or wages the best argument. It's only through spirit that we can see clearly the true facts without judgment, not the other way around. It's like putting the cart before the horse. People will recognize facts spoken without judgment. They will see from their hearts. Don't be fooled by their response, because spirit is touching them, they just don't know it. It's like this land. Maybe many moons from now, you will see how this land has changed you without you even knowing it."

"A Ho," I said.

Then, in an grand voice, Spotted Eagle said, "So I say to people out there who want to help themselves: Walk the path of spirit and what is needed will follow. Again, John, it's about trusting what you can't see with your eyes, only with your heart."

Spotted Eagle went on with another story. "I met this woman who told me the house next door to hers is owned by a very wealthy lady. She said this lady doesn't live there more than ten to twelve days a year because she has houses all over. And this woman tells me this wealthy lady is of great spirit. That's fine, she probably is of great spirit, but what is she doing with that spirit? What about all the homeless people? Some people, John, want to try to balance their conscience by doing what they think are good deeds, but what they're doing is only fooling themselves. They want it both ways. But God doesn't care about that; the true goodness inside you doesn't care about that. The good deeds won't pardon anything. God cares about acts of courage, and how much courage does it take to give money to people you think are more unfortunate? But who is more unfortunate? You know, those people may be poor but their spirit may be great. I'm sure you've heard of people who are dying and in the eyes of others are great people, are great successes. But when death is near and they reflect on themselves and look into their spirits, they find they've done nothing for that spirit. Maybe they were successful, as I said, in the eyes of people, but in the eyes of a higher being, they might not be thought of as successful."

"They keep hoping they'll change till their last breath," I added. My fear.

"That's right. Most people don't want to follow their true path," Spotted Eagle said. "They go to college and find out who's making the most money and follow them.

Why is it some doctors have to make half-a-million a year, sometimes more? Why is that necessary, especially when their supposed intentions are to help others? Each and every one of us has a different path, but in many ways they're parallel. In the old ways, there were some who were hunters, some who took care of the garden, and some who were arrow-makers or healers. That one chose to work with the tree because his hands were made for that. This one chose to be a messenger because he was swift of foot. But people follow money because it's what's used to place value on each individual. It's how we are assessed as human beings. And many people, no matter how much they know this to be true, are going to fight you about it. Again, if you admit to it, you will have to change, because living with it staring you in the eyes is too difficult. It may cause sickness, addictions, and true unhappiness. "My grandmother said this to me: 'In the future, the roots of all evil will be caused by mazsaka – money. When the time of the great change comes, let those with a family of six, who have thought so strongly of the dollar, who have devoted their lives to piling up money so they can think they're better than the next person – let them take a hundred dollar bill or a thousand dollar bill, sit down at their table when they're hungry, and see how far cutting that hundred dollar bill six ways takes away their hunger. It is the same with the precious metals they think are so powerful. Let them see how much an ounce of gold quenches their thirst.'"

"What do you tell those people who want to change, to follow their true path and go after what they really want to do in life?" I asked.

"It takes patience. So it takes twenty years to reach the height of your career, whatever it is – carpentry, teaching, writing, healing. But those twenty years, I can tell you, will be full of joy and rightness inside." Spotted Eagle pointed to his chest. Rightness – here was my word.

"John, I'm not saying anything that hasn't been said many times before." Spotted Eagle thought a moment. "I met a man who moved from a place he was happy. After a few years he wanted to move back. He said he had a lot of friends where he used to live and that he really loved the country. And he asks me what he can do. So I said, 'What's keeping you here?' And he says, 'What about money? What about my job?' This is the mind talking to him, and he knows it."

How many people did I know who faced this exact dilemma, including me.

"Approval is a big part of it," Spotted Eagle said. "People want others' approval to reassure them they're doing the right thing. But when you're acting from spirit, you won't feel the need for others' approval; here is a true sign you are on the path. Does everything have to be a success in the eyes of others? Can we just be satisfied we did something for ourselves – we got joy from it? Maybe you learned something, eh?"

"Yeah," I said quietly, almost in whisper.

Chapter Twenty

About a mile in front of us on the left side of the road, a range of jagged mountains came into sight. I studied them for a moment and then felt them pull at me – it was a physical sensation. I asked Spotted Eagle what the mountains were called.

"Badlands," Spotted Eagle said.

"Oh, yeah? I've heard of that place."

As we moved closer to them, that soft feeling came into my chest. Then my eyes just naturally looked up into the sky, and I saw a flock of birds, whose species I couldn't distinguish, moving in the directions of the Badlands. For some reason their flying in that direction seemed important to me. Surprisingly, I stayed quiet about sighting them. Then I turned my eyes to the front and found Black Hawk, twisted around in the front seat, peering at me. He stared into my eyes for a long moment. I sensed he was gauging something. Then he turned back to the front and exchanged a brief glance with Spotted Eagle.

I felt as if the entire moment of sighting the birds and Black Hawk's peering at me hadn't happened. Time seemed to stop, then start again. I was disoriented but still inside the feeling of spirit.

At the next exit we got off the highway and drove onto a two-lane service road toward the Badlands. As we neared them, that feeling in my chest deepened. I saw that they were not mountains but hills which resembled gigantic pale-red sand castles.

The road became a pass through them, winding higher and higher. Everything seemed so still. Small green valleys hid behind narrow passages and, except for the road, all seemed as it had hundreds of years ago. Why would I think that, I wondered.

For no reason, I turned to the right and there, in a shallow valley, a buck with small antlers was walking away from us.

"Over there," I yelled.

Black Hawk and Spotted Eagle turned to make me feel better, but I knew they had seen him before I had. The buck looked back and watched us pass. He peered at us as if he knew us.

"The buck turning to greet us in this place is all that is needed," Black Hawk proclaimed. His mood had turned solemn again. I wondered what he was thinking. I resisted asking him, for I sensed he was waiting for a time and a place to tell me many things he had felt and thought along the journey.

It occurred to me that I had finally spotted a relative.

Perhaps I was learning about the validity of faith and was listening inside for directions.

There was a physical pull to get out and walk around, and Spotted Eagle, as if reading my sensations, stopped about a mile later in a deserted rest area/lookout, and we got out. The wind was there again, stronger because of the increased elevation. I looked around and was awed by the silence and sensed I wasn't alone. Perhaps that's why the silence struck me as so unusual. It was as if I was in a silent room, crowded only with friends.

Black Hawk and Spotted Eagle peered down onto the plains. I went over and joined them.

"When the great bear rests his eyes and the geese journey south," Black Hawk said, "this is the time my people with their families journey over the plain to our winter camp." He pointed out across the plains. "The wind is at our back giving us strength, and when the wind blows across our face, we know it is healing us. This is the way. It is in these things we see the path of Tunkashila."

Black Hawk became another person with those words. I knew this was truly him, how he was in his time. The words resonated with an ancient knowing. For a brief moment, I felt transported back in time and connected with my ancestors, whoever they might be. I was link in a long chain. If you walked the path, I mused, was the gift a falling into place with the long line from the beginning?

We heard a dull roar in the distance. The sound was coming toward us. We all looked up into the sky, and four fighter jets in formation came into sight. They were over us in seconds, shattering the stillness, the beauty. It was the hunters in the woods again--an invading, brutal sound. I watched sadly as they disappeared quickly into the horizon. Like the missile silos, I thought. What was there to say? How did you talk to those in control about the senselessness of war and the machines it created? They just couldn't hear you. They only concerned themselves with shows of strength as a way of bringing peace. Why didn't they see the hypocrisy of that posture? Why did we – citizens of a democratic country – have to feel so helpless in getting anyone who could make changes to hear us from a place of openness? Why did it have to be more complicated than: war is wrong, creating bombs is wrong, just stop doing it? But they say it is more complicated, and they know better, right, because they're sitting across from our enemy and know how they will act. I wondered if the enemy was thinking the same thing about us, and if the enemy is capable of goodness, and if the enemy is made, as Spotted Eagle said, by the same hands. Do they all sit around and hope in their hearts that one day the other one will say, "Look, I'm completely disarming and stopping the production of any more bombs, and if you blow us up, okay, but at least we did what God would have wanted us to do."

I thought, How can anyone possibly believe God condones nuclear weapons? But what do they say at the end of a speech about defense? "God bless you and America."

Is it really about money and power and nothing more? Again, I was angry. But how could I see the use of nuclear weapons without judgment?

Even with my anger, I always came back to the same place – what can I do to stop what is just plain wrong, or, at least, what can I do to be heard? Is that the distinction, I contemplated? How do I define my contribution? Is that where I go awry, in the defining, as opposed to just concerning myself with the acts of contribution? Am I only focused on outcome and thus defeated before I start? Was this analogous to what the government does in relation to defense and nuclear war? And ultimately, was this what Spotted Eagle alluded to in "It is the act itself that has hurt us, not the details"? If we follow what is right in our hearts, will the details follow? Perhaps, yes.

We began to walk back to the car and Black Hawk turned to me. "These are things that can harm the earth?" He motioned to the sky, indicating the jets. "Yes. And people, they are built to kill people."

"The enemy?" he asked.

"Yes, I guess you could say that."

He stood for a second, mulling that over, then walked toward the car. I wondered why he asked about the enemy.

Spotted Eagle came up on my side.

"You know, in the old way," Spotted Eagle said, "man depended on his relatives to know when to travel, to fish, to hunt, to wed, to pray. These are the things Black Hawk spoke about before. Listen well, John. Machines weren't needed to tell of coming snows, buildings weren't needed to pray. It is in nature's relationship to itself that we see how to live. It is a reflection for us, eh?"

Spotted Eagle continued to catch me off guard with the

slant of his conversations. Sometimes they seemed to come from nowhere and not relate in the least to what we were talking about. I wondered if this was intentional? Was a conspiracy afoot?

We got back into the car and continued through the Badlands. I was reluctant to leave, for this place felt safe to me. I had the feeling that someday I would return to these silent hills, find a small cliff, and peer out across the earth. I knew this was my special place.

Chapter Twenty-One

After about an hour, we changed over to a service road which gradually began to move through a forest area. I had a sudden thought, and as I leaned over to confirm it, I knew by the expressions and energy they both emanated that I was right.

"Are we in the Sacred Hills?" I asked.

"Ho," Black Hawk said. He was proud that I had known.

"We call them Paha Sapa," Spotted Eagle added.

"Why are they called the Sacred Hills?" I asked.

"It is here my people came to pray. It is here my people were born from," Black Hawk said.

I felt the sadness again, but it was even stronger now. I almost wanted to run away from it, an opposite response to my familiar need to discover what it was about. I peered out at the landscape, which opened and closed from large meadows to thick wooded areas. I felt my features darken, my stare narrow. I didn't know what it was in response to.

Another spontaneous thought came to me. I asked Spotted Eagle, "Do your people still come here to pray?"

"Yes, even though the government has taken these Sacred Lands away from us, a small percentage of them do. These hills, the Black Hills as they call them, they say are rich with precious metals, and a great deal of money is made from tourists. They tell us that we would drive the tourists away, but this is untrue. The big corporations have come in here a little at a time and slowly taken over sections that are designated as National Forest Land. They're strip mining, which completely strips a hill of all living things. Look over there."

He pointed to an area about a mile in the distance. A large hill stood out among the others because, as he had said, it was completely devoid of all trees and vegetation; it was just brown dirt.

"That's one of them?" I asked.

"Yes," he said. Black Hawk also saw the hill, but I perceived no response from him, which again I thought strange. "We pray for these hills on our journey. We pray in our heart that one day the tree and grass may again cover them.

"Ho," I responded.

"You know, John, it's not so much the place you go to pray or offer thanks but the journey there that can be important," Spotted Eagle said.

I nodded, understanding, and was also glad he had reminded me.

"It's like the wind Black Hawk speaks about. It serves to remind us of change and how change has a purpose.

On a journey, if the wind blows against us, perhaps this is the time to rest and let its strength come into us and heal. When the wind blows behind us, perhaps this is the time to move forward with its force supporting us. These are lessons on a journey we can be reminded of, and, again, are only seen when you look with your heart."

Fir trees on both sides loomed over us as the road narrowed. I pictured myself wandering through the forest, finding a cave, and settling down to a nice uncomplicated existence with nature and the animals. I could put all these concerns about the world behind me. But, I concluded, this again is an escape and keeps me from facing the truth about our power to change ourselves and the world we live in. The problems seemed so insurmountable, though – the dreaded details again.

"In the Catholic religion, this is where Christ went to pray," Spotted Eagle said, indicating the forest. He surprised me in the mention of Catholicism. "But again those followers don't want to look at that fact, they don't want to make the connection. It's common sense, John, eh? If Christ went out to the woods or the desert to pray, then perhaps that is where we should pray – 'But what about our glamourous church which shows we're the true religion, we're the better religion, we're closer to God? Look at how much money we spend for his benefit.'"

I could hear the Catholics and my parents getting their Bibles out with these words. I was sure my folks would personally file the papers with the Vatican to have me excommunicated. Especially, when I told them what Spotted

Eagle had said made sense to me.

He went on, deepening my uneasiness. "Where is it that Christ said build tall buildings and make lots of money. In what book was that written? They should take a look at the books they call holy books. But what religion is the richest? What religion has the most money hidden in its coffers? Why? What war do they have to fight in this day and age to convince others that theirs is the right way, the true religion? This is a fact, John, but, eh, like the Indians, forgotten facts. This is why most religions cut out a belief in Mother Earth – how can you tax it? In their books, it says bring the words to them, not force it on them, not make them pay for it."

I nodded quietly; he was right. Forgotten were the times of popes leading battles, forging wars against nonbelievers and killing them. I had always found it difficult to understand the hypocrisy of any organized religion's adamancy that they are the true religion, the true path to God. Isn't it completely in opposition to the love of God they speak of, I had thought? Maybe I had been oversimplifying, but these inconsistencies were right on the surface and blatant. I now considered that perhaps only the courage not to be sucked into theoretical arguments is needed to bring them out in the open.

Black Hawk now appeared happier, it seemed to glow from inside him. He said, "Many seasons ago we came through that glade." He pointed to a small meadow off to the right. "We had traveled three, four days. Many hawks and eagles were with us. My grandfather said that the old ones looked over us for we traveled the way of the ancestors, and it was good. I did not understand this, for it was the path we took each season to the winter camp. But never had I seen our relatives so dark in the sky. 'What is different, grandfather?' I asked. 'Little one,' he said to me, `the way of the ancestors is not met by path or foot but by how we journey over that which is sacred – the earth, the rock, all the eye can see.' I nodded that I understood, but he said to me, 'Go, find a stone where you see the path no longer turns.' I walked down the path we had traveled for many seasons, and when it turned, I walked the opposite way. My eyes covered the ground, watching for a stone, but there were many stones…many stones." Black Hawk laughed.

"I returned and said, 'Grandfather, which stone do I pick, there are so many?' 'Yes, this is the way, my son.'" Black Hawk cracked up again. I was anxious to hear the punch line.

"I sat by the fire and thought on my grandfather's words. When I looked up, I saw his eyes watched over me like the great hawks. Soon I fell asleep and dawn came. Many seasons turned, and I had not found the meaning to my grandfather's words that day about the many stones. Many more seasons pass and as they do, before my heart, before my eyes, his words are spoken on the wind, on the light of the sun touching a small tree reaching to the sky and, John," he said softly, "I still have not seen the words. It is so. A Ho."

I felt sad and proud at his story. I didn't see its message about the stones either. But his feeling for his grandfather and the gift he was given stood for a lot in my eyes. Perhaps it represented trust, faith, and something else which I couldn't put my finger on. I was grateful he had told me, though. Then I wondered if that was it – gratitude.

Chapter Twenty-Two

It took us an hour to come out of the forest. The terrain evolved into rolling green hills. The sun began to set. Civilization crept up slowly – gas stations, various homes, and a commercial building here and there. I wondered if this area was still considered the hills and asked.

"Yes, John, but as you can see..." Spotted Eagle pointed to the cropping up of commercialism.

We drove into a one-street town bordered by stores, and as quickly as we came in, we were out. We passed by a row of suburban homes, then the land broke open again. After a couple of minutes spirit touched me inside in that now familiar way, centering around my chest and eyes. I sensed we were close to something.

A mile in the distance, I saw a small mountain surrounded by flat terrain. The mountain stood isolated as if it had just sprung up from the earth. I knew this was our destination. The silence in the car suddenly became charged.

Within five minutes we pulled up and stopped at the

base of the mountain. Black Hawk turned to me and said, "We are in the place of the ancestors, Ho."

"Ho," I responded.

I peered up at the four large hills comprising the mountain. It looked deserted, but I knew without doubt something mysterious and very powerful went on in there. We drove in through a gate, and I saw a sign designating the site as a park. Then we went by a closed information center. A few hundred yards above the center I saw a house. I asked Spotted Eagle who lived here.

"Ranger station," he said.

"Oh," was all I could think to say. Rangers?

We came to a road marked Authorized Personal Only, and without hesitation Spotted Eagle turned down it. We drove around a quick turn into an unpaved parking area which revealed an open valley escalating up to three peaks. We sat for a moment. I watched Black Hawk's face – he had been here before. I was surprised to see that Spotted Eagle also watched Black Hawk, and it was in that moment that I sensed Spotted Eagle let himself be guided fully and respectfully by Black Hawk's actions. Black Hawk got out slowly, and we followed. We walked in front of the car and looked across a stream at the valley which was dotted with the shells of dome-like structures. I asked Black Hawk what they were.

"Sweatlodges," he said. I had heard about people in Woodstock using them, but it didn't feel like the time to inquire into their purpose.

Black Hawk turned to Spotted Eagle and nodded, signaling something. Spotted Eagle went to the trunk of the car and took out an old wooden box. He opened it, brought out a small blanket, and unrolled it flat on the ground. Then he reached in the box and lifted out an ancient pipe about two and a half feet in length which he laid gently on the blanket. Then two deer-skin pouches went next to the pipe. He rolled everything securely up in the blanket. Spotted Eagle and I walked over to Black Hawk who had stayed at the front of the car, studying the valley.

Suddenly, a pickup truck, kicking up dust, drove rapidly into the parking area. A young guy in uniform in his early twenties jumped out. I imagined this was the ranger.

"Sorry, you guys, but the park closes at dusk." the ranger said across to us.

Spotted Eagle jumped right in, as if this had happened before, "We'll be camping the night."

"Do you have a permit?" the ranger asked.

"We don't need a permit," Spotted Eagle said quietly.

"Well, I'm sorry, sir, but a permit is necessary."

I couldn't believe it, asking Indians for a permit on their sacred ground. To my surprise, Black Hawk stood calmly and appeared as if whatever the problem it would be worked out.

"You're talking about paying money to camp here?" Spotted Eagle asked.

"Yes, that's the policy." The ranger started to get impatient.

"Well, son, let me ask you a question. Are you a religious person?" Spotted Eagle asked in a soft manner, hard to ignore.

After much hesitation, the ranger said, "Yeah."

"Say if you went to church and someone stood outside and asked you to pay to get in, how would you feel?"

He didn't have an answer for this, and Spotted Eagle went on. "See, for us, this is our church. Our ancestors have been coming here for hundreds of years. They have walked the path that you and I now stand on." When he said "path we stand on," it sent a chill up my back. Then the sadness came over me again.

"Sir, I can understand how you feel, but we have rules here."

"Well, we've come a long way." I felt as if Spotted Eagle not only referred to this moment but to the history of his people. "I know in your heart you can see what I speak about. It's difficult to take a chance on your fellow human beings, no matter how much we want to. But we will go to the place where the great chiefs of my people have come to offer thanks for the life they were given and the lives of all who walk the earth. We will do this thing. I hope that you can find it in your heart to let us pass. For this is the way."

Like me, the ranger was blown away. I summoned all my strength to keep the tears from coming.

The ranger shuffled around in the dirt caught between anger, frustration, and confusion. He examined me and then Black Hawk, I think he was searching for something to get hold of, for some opening to sneak through with face saved.

"I'm going to have to talk to my superiors," he said, then walked back to his truck, feigning a focused purpose. I wasn't angry at him or resentful, only sad for the whole damn state of affairs in this country that a conversation like this had to take place. He drove off in the direction of the ranger station.

"We can go. He will not return. His heart speaks too loudly," Spotted Eagle said. He was right; he didn't come back.

Spotted Eagle waited for Black Hawk to make the first step toward the small bridge crossing the stream.

Black Hawk peered up at the sky, and my eyes followed. Twilight sent a red glow over the horizon. He seemed to absorb the energy from the sky. He waited another brief moment then walked across the bridge. We followed in silence.

I landed my foot on the earth of other side, and an ancient feeling flowed into my body and spirit. I walked, and the feeling became stronger. This ancient presence didn't feel focused in any particular point, but seemed to exude in a wave coming from the whole mountain. Here was a small pocket of honor among the disturbances of our age.

We moved slowly, respectfully toward the center where the shell of a sweatlodge stood. I paid particular attention to where and how I walked ever so softly. We continued up for about a hundred yards, passing remnants of campfires and two more hulks of sweatlodges, then Black Hawk stopped in a small, naturally enclosed area. A small, treed knoll on one side shielded us from the parking lot, and on the other side was the base of one of the four peaks, fronted by a stream.

Black Hawk motioned humbly for us to sit down. He sat facing me and Spotted Eagle was to my right. We quieted ourselves and took what I felt was an intentional waiting moment to show respect for this sacred spot; this was a place to not rush into anything. After five minutes, Spotted Eagle unwrapped the rolled blanket and set on it the pipe, pouches, and a small flat stone, four inches in diameter.

The pipe ceremony followed. When Spotted Eagle shared the pipe with us, and I drew the smoke into my mouth, I wondered, Am I now part of what I have so relentlessly fought against. Forces that wished to be my friends called my true nature, the goodness, the God inside of me.

I mirrored Spotted Eagle's and Black Hawk's movements with the pipe. It was an action that for some unknown reason drove the connections between man into me. I began to see with these insights, how insights were sometimes manifested from unknown, unsuspecting, and indirect origins.

I felt privileged to share the pipe with Spotted Eagle and Black Hawk. Were there more warriors such as these in our day and age? I answered, yes, for now I might see them if I stayed on the path.

Whenever I forget what needs to be protected, I will hold close Spotted Eagle's words at the beginning of the ceremony: "Hear me, Great Spirit, I, Spotted Eagle of the Nakota Sioux, the Mother Tribe, Protectors of the Sacred Stone Quarry, call to you." And with those words he had begun.

(I have left out, upon their request and my full agreement, the specifics of the scared pipe ceremony. The reasons are more fully explained further on.)

We finished the ceremony, and without reason I looked up in the sky and saw that two eagles circled directly above us. I had never seen an eagle before. They are big! The wing span is staggering.

"It is said," Spotted Eagle ruminated, "that if you have lived a good life and have stayed on the path inside your heart, you will return as an eagle or a hawk and watch over a sacred place." An eagle, a hawk, I mused. Oh, how it would be to fly!

We watched the eagles as they floated over us. Night was settling quickly. Spotted Eagle started to build a fire with wood and kindling lying around our position. Black Hawk had been silent for some time and reflected those subtleties that indicated he was home. But something about the way in which he sat and moved seemed familiar to me.

"All is as it should be," he stated, peering at the eagles. "Our path and journey have been strong with spirit. Ho."

We sat in quiet for a while. I breathed more easily with the silence as it wrapped itself around me. I think my two friends sensed my balance and had other lessons and known secrets to offer.

Spotted Eagle began, "You know, John" – it was always – "you know, John." I began to get the hint – "the individual has to just stand up and be counted, eh?" He laughed, knowing he quoted someone or other, and added, "Maybe just counted by himself."

By himself, I thought. Yes.

Spotted Eagle went on. "If you ask, `What can I do? What I can do?' then you are already defeated. As I was saying about people reading the books that have been written, people also have to see the individual can make a difference. This is a fact, John. History has proven this over and over again. But like everything we have talked about, people don't want to believe this fact. Even as they read about history with their own eyes, they don't make the connection between the person they're reading about and themselves. It's so much easier not too, eh?"

Then suddenly, both their eyes bore into me.

"You, John, don't make the connection," Spotted Eagle leveled.

"What do you mean?!"

There was no response from them, only serious, unbending expressions. I disliked my defensive feelings, which was unusual for me; I truly wanted to be rid of them. But for the first time, I saw the innocence of them. I thought a moment then said, "Maybe you're right…I mean…I'm willing to look at this with an open mind!"

We laughed.

"Like the fire we have spoken about – one spark," Black Hawk said. He outlined the fire with his hands, fluttering them toward the heavens. "It is in this way we see the path," he repeated, smiling.

I quieted myself. I felt the wind across my face and stared up at the dense stars which seemed to surround me from all sides. My soul was again suddenly at peace. The feeling of serenity felt so right. Perhaps I hastened back to it because I just wasn't willing to give it up anymore. I watched the fire, isolating the flames until I felt pulled inside the yellow and red colors, absorbed by the universe of the fire. I sailed on a journey through the colors of the four races mingling together. What Black Hawk and Spotted Eagle had said suddenly penetrated in that deeper, clearer way. I saw that the fire was an example and reflection, or perhaps a map of the path of spirit. I saw that reflections and the sign posts of how to walk the path of spirit were in nature's interaction with itself, or in this case, the interaction of the different colored flames. I told myself to watch how the birds interacted with each other or how water supported the earth. These were all separate but the same. They were unsuspecting places to look for guidance and only seen if we dropped our frames of reference and beliefs. If we opened our eyes, we might see what was in front of us.

It does go round and round, I thought. I wondered if that was what Spotted Eagle was indicating when he had drawn the imaginary circle? The sadness was on me suddenly. Did the sadness have something to do with the circle? Was I coming around? Was I COMING BACK? This place? THIS PLACE! That pine tree over there and the stream…I'VE BEEN HERE BEFORE!

I jumped up and ran back and forth aimlessly, frantically peering at boulders, bushes, the ground, the sky, the stars. YES, I HAVE BEEN HERE. I hadn't made the "connection" in more ways than one! YES, and hadn't Black Hawk said to me within the first few seconds of meeting him that I had been to Dakota.

I stopped. I wanted to grab hold of my past, but how could I get closer to it? How many hundreds of years ago had I sat in this sacred place and touched the clouds and the earth underneath me? How long? I was back home now, a home inside. Why did it feel that way, I wondered? Could it be the remembering itself was the only gem to see, the only home to see?

I looked down at Black Hawk and Spotted Eagle facing each other. They were silent, intense, centered, powerful. I slowly sat down on my spot. I faced them, raised my palm, stretched my fingers as wide as they would go, and spoke these words, "Hau Kola."

They, warriors, each in turn, raised their hands and said, "Hau Kola."

I remembered what it meant: Greetings Friend, Greetings Brother.

Chapter Twenty-Three

"When we met in Woodstock, John, did sadness fall over your heart?" Black Hawk asked me. I nodded, shocked he knew. The meaning of the sadness had finally come clear to me. It was a falling sadness over my heart about the changes in the world, from the time I sat here in this sacred place hundreds of years ago until this day. But also a sadness from having forgotten my past.

"It was a reflection of my heart and our brother Spotted Eagle," Black Hawk told me.

"Ho," came out of my heart. They both smiled, proud. Their moments of pride in me made me happy. They knew I had discovered part of my past. Nothing more needed to be said.

"From the time of my people a great change has come," Black Hawk said. "This is the way. And so a change will come again. It is so. I had lost this knowing, John. On our journey its light is once again in my heart, and the sadness is no more."

"Is that why you weren't angry at the many things we

have seen?" I asked.

"What has stood before we walked? What will stand after?" Black Hawk asked me.

"The earth, nature."

"Yes. And what is given to us from Tunkashila?"

"Spirit."

"Ho. Spirit is the way. This, as children of Tunkashila, is what we have to offer each other. Only spirit."

"War with any people is a road that has no end," said Spotted Eagle, looking at me and also Black Hawk. "If you have anger in your heart it is a road that goes nowhere. Change can't come from anger, any anger, John."

"Some wars can't be helped," I said, suddenly defensive.

I say this to you from my heart" said Spotted Eagle – "let those who act in this way have what their minds want, for it will give them no peace."

"I don't understand what you're saying! You mean if someone should attack us, we should let them have what they want?"

"Those are details, John," Spotted Eagle said forcefully. "What are these details in a thousand years, in ten thousand years? What do these details matter when we don't know what tomorrow brings?" He continued to include Black Hawk in his attention. I thought this strange. "To break the circle of war that you see and the many who walk the earth see. One warrior will stand with courage and trust in what he can't see. He will trust in Tunkashila, and the way God has given us will be once more. A way of love, of peace. But this way can't be seen if this warrior's eyes only see the details, only see with judgment. Details may stand over him and laugh. Details may speak to him of his rightness, but this is an illusion. If we fight for what we feel belongs to us, aren't we like those who fight against us? To free yourself from thoughts that are not spirit is the greatest gift you give your people. It is a gift to your own spirit."

Black Hawk looked perplexed, I saw that he had been listening intently to Spotted Eagle's words.

"Someday someone will stand and the circle of mind will be broken," said Spotted Eagle. "But many people become caught because they don't see results, eh? It's taken many hundreds of years to come to this place, and so it will returning. But when that person stands, John, he will see the future and not fear. He will see the innocence of the mind and how those who live from the mind are only keeping themselves from what we all truly want."

"To live in peace," I offered.

"How do we live in peace, John?" Spotted Eagle asked. "By living in peace now. Not by fighting for it, eh? Fighting for it in any way – even with words."

"I don't understand," I said frantically. "Aren't words of peace good?"

"Speak of peace by example. Remember?" Spotted Eagle asked.

"Yes?"

"It's the same. Words of peace have been spoken for many years. This, again, is history. Do we have peace? No. What is there to speak about when the only answer is to live in peace?" Spotted Eagle laughed at his own words.

He was thoroughly enjoying himself. "We must speak with peace in our actions. Only in this place can the words of truth be spoken and heard, not the other way. Cart before the horse, eh?"

"I guess I see what you're trying to say but the reality of it escapes me."

"There you go." Spotted Eagle smiled, and added, "Here is an example."

Where is an example, I wondered? Am I an example? I peered at him. Yeah, I was the example! Wrong listening! But I went ahead anyway.

"What I'm trying to say is the reality of, say, a threat of war."

"In those moments, you must have faith in spirit, have faith in God, have faith in what you can't see," Spotted Eagle said. "If my people, the Sioux, were to walk the earth no more, my spirit would still be happy if the clear waters ran over the earth and the leaves still fell from the Grandfather Trees. All this would bring a smile to my heart because I know I am part of that tree and part of that water. To live in spirit with each breath. This is what you're looking for. This is the way."

"This is the way." He kept repeating this. What he said was certainly radical, I thought, almost appeared insane, but the natural common sense I was remembering kept shouting up at me, "Yes, yes, that's exactly right." No wonder they harped on getting me to listen with spirit. His words of having faith in the face of attack were the ultimate and perhaps final button in my mind to push. If such a thing had been spoken to me two days ago, my latent nationalism would have attacked. Now, even though I didn't totally agree, I could honestly see a glint of what they were trying to say. When I tried to picture a nation unwilling to enter into wars no matter how threatened it might appear, willing only to concern itself with living in peace in this breath, a spark of excitement shot through me. Oh, what a possibility! But so definitively idealistic. Many would say I was hallucinating.

"But we must survive, this is the way," Black Hawk said suddenly to Spotted Eagle.

"Yes, my brother, to protect those we love is part of who we are as human beings. But it is how we protect them that concerns Creator. There must be change, there must be growth from the old ways. I do not judge these ways. But to kill the children of Creator, even though they are our enemy, and they would try to kill us, I believe is not what Creator intended. Ho."

Black Hawk took a moment then said, "These words are strong, Spotted Eagle, I will let my heart rest with them. Ho."

I listened to their exchange and was impressed by the way Black had received Spotted Eagle's advice. It had never occurred to me to ask Black Hawk about how, in his era, he dealt with the enemy, or in other words, other tribes the Sioux were not on good terms with. But even with Spotted Eagle's counsel I was still unclear on what action to take. And I again fell into the hole of what I can do, the individual do. Spotted Eagle had said that when one says this, one is already defeated. This is certainly the truth, I reflected. I looked up at them with my concerned face, and, of course, without fail:

"One spark, John," said my brother, Black Hawk.

"Do you see, John, how everything we have spoken about is the same?" Spotted Eagle asked.

I shook my head.

"War of any kind. War with other nations. War with friends. War with yourself. Everything we have spoken about is the same but different, eh? You can only see clearly the way to peace from living your life in peace. It's like governments who say we live in peace. But how I define war is different. An action that is not of spirit, that is not of peace in this breath, is war. Weapons exist to kill. Why? Fear, control, mind."

Black Hawk and Spotted Eagle spoke these opinions with lightness in contrast to the heaviness of my thoughts and listening. I speculated that perhaps here was an example of what Black Hawk referred to as making change through a feeling of softness as opposed to the righteous anger I felt now and in the sixties. Perhaps that anger was innocent. How much would I have grasped or resisted if they had spoken their observations and insights to me with righteousness? I would have fought them every step of the way, perhaps turned away. But their lightness, laughter, and lack of judgment had attracted me to their insights. Yes, had made them accessible, for I hadn't felt threatened.

Spotted Eagle laughed. "What applies to government also applies to you!" Then in a big voice to the heavens he shouted, "Let the winds blow as they will, for they are of

Tunkashila as we are. This I pray."

Insights were coming to me rapidly, and with each one I felt close to the brink of seeing the answer to the question that I had been seeking from the beginning – how can the individual make a difference?

"Like the government, we as individuals spend a lifetime trying to control outcomes, eh?" Spotted Eagle went on to say. "Let the winds blow as they may. If you see the circle of your acts, see the sameness, you will find the power, the answer!"

I began to interpret Spotted Eagle's words with my mind, trying to see that missing piece. I caught myself and tried to quiet down.

"You are not alone on your journey, have you sought to know of this?" Black Hawk smiled.

"Ho." I smiled.

"When you know this in your heart, you will find solace," Spotted Eagle added. "We all truly want the same thing – to find the spirit inside ourselves, to walk with happiness and freedom from the mind. All people want this, John, and all people struggle in many different ways to get it, whatever they may be."

"Yes, and in the last twenty years there has been a new consciousness starting in the world," I said. "Many people are trying to help themselves, trying to get it together. They talk of spirituality and try to live in that way. A lot of books have been written and movements organized; it seems to be helping. They call it New Age, and, I think, it's a step in the right direction. I've even heard of people using sweatlodges in Woodstock." I pointed to the skeleton of one.

"Yes, I have seen this," Spotted Eagle said, "and read many of the books and talked with many people who try to follow a way of spirituality. And what I see is that they must, as Black Hawk says, 'live each breath in spirit.' And some have not been doing this. They have what I call an intellectual spirituality. This is not the way to happiness, and they, themselves, are aware of this."

He was mirroring some of my thoughts over the years about myself and the whole New Age movement, but doing it without my tone of venomous judgement.

Spotted Eagle went on. "What disturbs me, John, are some of these people who call themselves medicine men or women, or spiritual leaders. They talk about how to build shields, sing the sacred songs of my people, and describe other ceremonies they have no business talking about. These people – and I say this with love and softness in my heart, because again, their actions are innocent – are leading people down the wrong path. Even though they speak that technique is not important, they go ahead and talk about it in detail. Again, like the government, eh? They say this, but do that! What is important is the intention of spirit behind the details. Few talk about this. How can you sell spirit, John, eh? But these teachings of technique…?

"Intention of spirit is what needs to be learned, not how to build a shield, become one with your spirit animal, or to do a sweat. I tell you, John, the pipe I have sat for many seasons before I felt worthy of it, worthy of the gifts it could bring. Because I would not have seen those gifts.

"I have met people who say they want to follow a way of spirit. But where they go wrong," Spotted Eagle said, looking directly at me, "is they want spirituality now, this minute. What does that tell you?"

Was this true about me? I suppose it was. I felt relieved to know this and this reaction was a surprise in itself. Usually upon that type of nagging perceptive confrontation I would attack.

"You, John, as we all are, are guilty of wanting it now, although we are not truly guilty but, again, innocent. Innocent as those who write and talk of spirit, of God, only for money. Innocent as those who travel and charge hundreds of dollars to teach ways of the Indian people that they have no business teaching. If they were talking and acting from spirit, they would know it may take lifetimes to see truly the gift of a sacred ceremony or dance, not a weekend."

I had heard of these "weekend" workshops.

"I have known great men, elders in their eighties, who don't feel worthy or ready to seek a Vision Quest. But I watch these people, who call themselves medicine men or shamans, lead the young and old on a Sacred Vision Quest, or what they call a Vision Quest. But even this they do with mind, so people will give them money. John, a Vision Quest is eight days of fasting, filled with many prayers, offerings, and intention of giving something back. First, four days of sweats and prayers, then four days alone in one spot, not wandering around the hills. But they make it shorter and easier so people will buy it, eh?

"See, you have to look at their intentions, it is as simple as that. You must follow a path of spirit to have a right to what has been handed down from my ancestors and their ancestors. As children of Tunkashila, we see that only spirit is needed, and this technique or this tool is worth nothing without spirit. Building a shield, John, or saying a word over and over again simply will not lead you to spirit, will not bring you to the happiness and freedom you desire.

"People who call themselves Medicine People, or what I have seen lately, call themselves apprentices, are only fooling themselves. You see, in their titling, they are right from the start speaking from mind, seeking importance, seeking another road of illusion to give them security. They have to ask themselves honestly why they call themselves this person's apprentice.

"This year, Indian ways are popular. They meet someone who says they're a medicine person and suddenly they're an apprentice. But what are they next year? What will be `in' next year, eh? If I were to guide someone constantly, I wouldn't be taking care of their spirit. That person would not be following their own path, they'd be following mine. When I die, what do they do? When they come to the end of my moccasin track and my shell with my bones are laying there, what do they do? They're still in the same position they were in when they met me because they haven't learned to trust in themselves. I'd rather have these people learn one thing from me, and that is, to live their own lives, to realize we are all individual spirits and should run our lives that way.

"John, it's like the very rich we have spoken about. They try to balance their lives by giving to the poor. It's also the same with some people who say they lead a spiritual life. They have to take a look at their day to day lives, and see if it is a life of spirit. Ask themselves, are they like the rich, leading two lives, one of mind and one they think is spirit? The details may be different, John, for each individual. It could be a job you know you shouldn't be doing, or a place you don't want to live, or maybe you're around others you know aren't good for you. We each hide from spirit in our own way. And like you, we all know when this is so."

"The world needs more people living in spirit and less people talking about it," I said rhetorically, including myself as a talker and thinker.

Suddenly, a short gust of wind blew over us.

"Ho, our relative has offered its agreement," Black Hawk said. We all smiled in confirmation.

"As I said, the government and individuals are the same," Spotted Eagle repeated. "How can we speak against what we do ourselves? How we can know how to speak to what we want to change if we don't ourselves change? Example, John, eh? How can everything I say now be truly heard and understood if it's not listened to with spirit and spoken with spirit?"

The wind began to blow in strong gusts, pulling the flames higher toward the stars. Spotted Eagle added, "To listen with spirit and to see spirit in all things."

To see love in all things. How I wished I could in every

moment. Spotted Eagle hesitated for a long minute and then spoke words that opened a door inside me. They were words, spoken like Black Hawk's, with a separate world behind each one.

"John, it is in the recognition of our reflection in all things that we see the way--to recognize ourselves."

Isn't this what I had felt back in Woodstock, a recognition of myself in Black Hawk?! Didn't it quiet my doubts about the outrageousness of his being from the past? Didn't I feel the recognition when I followed him from the start? YES!

The wind seemed to blow directly over me, matching my feeling. I wanted to fly with its force.

Black Hawk spoke across to me. "We are all of spirit, John, remember?" Almost his first words. He had given it to me from the jump.

I nodded and said, "The trees, the little plants, the rock people, the four legged, the winged, all the two-legged of all races, are all of God."

"Ho. Who in their heart truly believes God chooses one race over another?" Spotted Eagle said.

"Yes, who in the depth of his soul doesn't know that?" I echoed. "Who could rationalize our equality away? If we let ourselves see our equality, all would be of peace."

We were quiet a moment. In the silence, Spotted Eagle's words about recognizing ourselves seemed to wash over me like a gentle wave and deepen my feeling of spirit. I looked up to find them watching me with what seemed to be an expression of recognition and amusement. I wondered what they knew. The way in which they looked at me seemed familiar. WAIT A MINUTE! Black Hawk had looked at me in that manner when we were in Woodstock; it was the expression I could never interpret. They seemed to be reading my thoughts and smiled even wider at me. I smiled back and laughed at our mutual smiling. Then as if the door had opened wider in front of me, it came clear to me – They were getting a kick out of seeing a past reflection of themselves in me! Black Hawk had witnessed a part of himself, and it had surprised him. History again, if we would only open our eyes and look! I was his history, as is a person we each encounter every so often, a person or a bit of history where we can learn of our innocence, learn of compassion for others and for ourselves. It is our witnessing of our own reflection that lets us see without judgment. We see our humanness and our connection to man. It was a circle.

Then, as if it were coming slowly at me from a hazy distance, I felt suddenly that maybe this recognizing, this opening of our eyes, could be the way to make a difference. But that was too conceptual, my mind shouted from the back. How did it translate into practical actions?

I wanted to ask them – to get their help – I was too close. The only question was, how to ask them! I looked down at the ground, laughing a bit to myself at my quandary. The laughing was a change for me. I think I was perhaps laughing at the determination and stick-to-itiveness of my mind, or even better, the stick-to-itiveness I gave it! Questions and more questions – that was what I really laughed at – my own willfulness. I just pointed my will in the wrong direction! I burst out with a loud laugh, and Black Hawk and Spotted Eagle imitated my suspicious, paranoid looks. I felt much better suddenly, and once again the feeling of spirit was with me. All need for one final question was suddenly gone. It was in this place of quiet where they wisely waited to speak to me, and they told me what I wanted to know.

"John, during our journey, you have seen many of the answers you have wanted – you have seen. Is this so?" Black Hawk Eagle asked.

The whole area around us suddenly became charged with sound as the wind rushed wildly through the trees, and howled between the peaks above. Had I seen the answers? Was this true? Something stood in the way of my vision, it felt like a weathered, broken-down fence ready to crumble.

I looked to them, and they both smiled.

"Our mind wants others to tell us, John, yes?" Spotted Eagle asked with his usual mischief.

NO, WHY WOULD I WANT OTHERS TO TELL ME, I yelled through my head! And at my obvious internal panic, Black Hawk placed his hand gently against his chest – listen with spirit – yes, yes, thanks. Spotted Eagle waited again for me to quiet down. I took a breath, closed my eyes for a moment, and felt the earth under me and the sky above. He went on.

"Then we can make them responsible, eh, for our victories and defeats? We need approval for what we know, then we don't have to believe in ourselves. Our mind thinks the answer comes from outside. We have to trust in ourselves,

John. Then we will see that we have the power to help ourselves, and this fact changes our lives. We are no longer able to blame others for our feelings, for our misfortunes. With trust, we receive what we want – freedom, peace. In the act of trust, in an act of spirit."

Trust in ourselves, I thought. There were moments over the last two days when I had asked myself, I had asked my spirit, and I had asked my instinct. And in my asking, I had seen the natural facts clearly. It's true, I just didn't trust myself. I didn't believe I could have the wisdom to know the right direction.

Then Spotted Eagle floored me. "John, you must let go of the struggle of not knowing, for you do know, as we all do. The struggle of not trusting."

YES, YES, YES, the struggle of not knowing. It was familiar wasn't it?! Uncomfortable but familiar. It was the familiarity with THE STRUGGLE TO KNOW that kept me bound in, kept me at a distance from the unknown, the feared place. But it was never a matter of not fearing it but of seeing that it wasn't the place I believed. See it with spirit and all will change.

Excitement shot through me. The wind, my brother, roared through the trees, and my spirit seem to expand and shoot to the stars and back. A weight felt as if had lifted from my shoulders, from my heart.

It occurred to me that perhaps, like the unknown, we had to understand and see making a difference from a place of spirit, also. Subsequently redefine it. Perhaps we make differences in ways we aren't aware of? Perhaps we assess our ability to make a difference through the mind, and this defeats us?

WERE THESE EXAMPLES? I thought suddenly. Examples of my ability to arrive at insights on my own. I continually worded them as questions, doubts, speculation. I didn't BELIEVE IN MYSELF, in my ability to come to the truth myself.

I smiled inside. We must live each breath in spirit and then look. Not look and then try to find spirit. The cart before the horse.

I looked up at my two brothers, and as I did, they moved their spirit inside the storm of wind surrounding us. It gathered strength from our spirit, as we gathered strength from it.

I knew in my heart that the time to leave was close. I looked into the eyes of Spotted Eagle and Black Hawk and saw they had the same feeling. The journey to Woodstock was upon us. But it was not a journey back, for I would not return to the same place. I knew that through my spirit I had changed; the world had changed.

A cry pierced the roar of wind, "PEEEEE." A black hawk swept down from the sky and came to rest in front of us, his head high with dignity. Black Hawk remained still. The hawk let out another cry in greeting, "PEEEEE."

From the opposite direction, I heard a similar cry, felt a similar feeling but ever so different. With wings of incredible proportions, an eagle floated down out of the darkness and landed opposite the hawk – a spotted eagle. How beautiful and majestic he was – how complete he looked. What an excitement, to know, to feel that we were made from the same hands and were of the same spirit. To think about all we could learn from such an example, such a reflection. Spotted Eagle greeted him with a commanding sweep of his hand, and the eagle cried out in formal greeting.

I called inside my heart to my brother the deer. I saw a flash of fur cross the stream, and, ever so gently, with sureness, with a regality, the buck approached us. He stopped in front of me, and I raised my hand. In his eyes I felt the eternal connection between us.

Spotted Eagle and Black Hawk shouted to the sky, to the Sacred Mountain, to Tunkashila. I could not hear their words through the wind, but I knew them to be of thanks and offerings for all that had been given to us.

My words of thanks, like theirs, carried into the wind; they spoke of my wanting to give something back. I hoped they were enough for all the precious gifts that had been offered me.

We were leaving this sacred place, but I knew it would always live in my heart. I had returned and been given the precious gift of remembering. I prayed that I would continue to nurture it. I also knew this journey was not over. We were to travel to a place I wanted to return to, and I would see with my new eyes or my old eyes that I had remembered. I don't know how, but I knew reflections rested in that place.

The same wind that caressed my face now had touched me in that first moment in Woodstock. My brothers' eyes locked with mine and in one breath we were inside the wind. I was my spirit animal, and flanking me, were the eagle and hawk. We traveled up to the sky without time and speed and broke through into the womb of Mother Earth that Black Hawk and I had passed though. It soothed me, prepared me, deepened the roots of my spirit, and then the earth transformed into the clear fresh water of the waterfall's pool. We swam to the surface, and without another motion, stood on the shore next to one another with our spirit animals by our side. We looked across at the waterfall. It was the way we had come, yes. We glided smoothly through trees, and as before, there stood the cabin. Then, as if transitions did not exist, we found ourselves inside the cabin, standing across from our human forms. No words were spoken, there was only a passing feeling that we would once again return here. This place would remain if we believed.

I turned to the door, and only my turn was needed to feel the trees brush against me as we traveled through the woods. My eyes were the buck's, and the eagle and hawk flew above me. Without an extra motion, our spirits soared to the sky. The clouds enfolded us, softening even more the edges of my heart. Then it was the whiteness again. I was moving, though in a way that was beyond any capacity to understand; I was the movement, only that. I followed behind my brothers as we broke through and felt the water of the lake that had beckoned me down, a day ago – a hundred years ago. Here was the lake of the lesson I had not seen yet, like Black Hawk with his grandfather's story. We came to the surface, and before us was the forest outside Woodstock.

I peered at the shore with the knowing eyes of the deer – "Could I see that all was possible from here?" – yes, all was truly possible.

I knew where I wanted to go. My soul touched the spirit there and filled with the feeling of love I had felt there so many years ago. Intention was all that was needed. In a rush of land beneath me and a breath, we were there. The earth of the farm was under our feet in the dawn light. The earth I stood on for three days those many years ago, next to half million brothers and sisters – Yasgir's farm, site of the Woodstock Concert.

Spotted Eagle and Black Hawk stood silently beside me. To show them this place, to share it with them, meant all to me.

"This is the place of the gathering," proclaimed Black Hawk.

"Ho," I responded.

"We have come to the place of the Sacred Hoop where all races have been one," said Spotted Eagle.

"It is so," I said.

I looked to the place where the stage sat, and I listened for the music of feeling, power, and simplicity. I had come back here almost every year since I had moved to Woodstock, and each year the memory of the music had become fainter and fainter. The feeling I had while I leaned against that big tree, listening to Jimi Hendrix, had felt close to being extinguished forever. I could now hardly hear the singing of Janis Joplin and all the others – so many of them. They had all come – all the great groups.

I motioned humbly for my two brothers to sit and, as we had in South Dakota, we sat across from one another. I peered around at the empty space and tried to imagine the faces of the thousands who had covered the land, as Black Hawk had said, like buffalo. This was my ritual each time I came back. The sadness was on me as it always was. I suppose that each time I tortured myself with it. The pain became familiar to me, and I wrapped it around me. It was safe inside there, I knew what to expect. I was surprised that the familiar sadness penetrated through my new-found strength and good feelings. Spotted Eagle, reading my obvious expression offered some guidance.

"John, if you hold this place in sadness, you will put up a wall to the possibility of it happening again. On our journey it has become clear to me that I too held much in sadness. But spirit isn't about sadness; it is about joy."

"I, like my brothers, have learned of sadness," Black Hawk said, surprising me. "It is with joy that a great fire can grow and all can be possible."

"We had many dreams then," I said with a positive tone. "Yes, and those dreams are still there, John. Open yourself to dreaming them again," Spotted Eagle advised.

It is needed," Black Hawk added.

"I guess I fear the disappointment," I responded.

"Where does fear come from?" Black Hawk asked. I remembered the lesson from the mountain we had climbed together. Once again he had given it to me from the jump.

"From the mind," I answered, smiling.

"Ho, let the winds blow as they may. Outcomes, John,"

Spotted Eagle said and added, "There was friendship in this place."

"Friendship without wanting. This is of spirit," Black Hawk said.

"Yes, there was," I said. "We all helped each other. Even the older people who lived in the area gave us food and support. It was a feeling of unity."

"You know," Spotted Eagle began. "Maybe a long time ago, like at the concert, there was a gathering of many races here. Perhaps something very strong happened here, and that's why it happened again. So it rests now, waiting to rise up. And when it does, perhaps this time we won't have to use the drugs and liquor to deaden the mind. I, in no way, condone the use of drugs, John, but with their use, they deadened the consciousness, the mind, and the fear of other races taught to them by society. You see, when the mind was quiet, the spirit came out. But the mind woke up again, eh, and it became scared. The mind could see how it had acted, and that it was possible to live in harmony, love, and peace with other races. This fact scared the hell out of it! So maybe the next time they won't have to use drugs and people will have clear minds. Then the mind and spirit can work together to live in peace with all of God's children."

"You know, you're right," I said. "The drugs helped in the moment, but it didn't give me the belief I could feel that way without them, just on my own. There was no act of trust, no act of walking on the path of spirit. We've had two revival concerts but they were both too commercial with no feeling of the old spirit."

"Woodstock, John, is just a feeling of love, of spirit, eh? It's not only in this sacred place, it can happen anywhere." Spotted Eagle laughed, circling his hand all around us. "Look for the Woodstock in all things, look for the balance because that's what you had here. A long long time ago, my people and others, lived in balance and equality. It was a time when wanting to be better than your fellow human was not even a passing thought. These times can be once again, as our brother says, with one spark. You have to know, John, many people out there feel the same way you do. Many people want this equality again. We are all children of God, people of all religions. They call the Creator different names, but this doesn't matter, only if you want it to!"

Spotted Eagle was thoroughly enjoying himself. I listened with gladness in my heart.

"See, John, when a person's faith weakens, for whatever reason, instead of just seeing it with innocence, with love, he tries to make himself feel better by feeling superior to those of other religions. Then there are wars and negativity. Hate becomes our teacher. There must be joy in the act of having faith. Here stands a warrior – in the act of. Ho."

"Ho," I echoed, grateful.

I peered across the farm. My half-million friends no longer looked back at me, but something else did – their spirit. Like the woods in Woodstock, I could see their spirit, see the love. We honored life by giving something back in those three days--our love for life. We knew it was a gift from God. I had looked for the faces and the way it was and forgotten what was truly important--the spirit. It would always live here. The memories, the details had trapped me.

"My brothers, you have honored me," Spotted Eagle said. There was a note of finality in his voice. "Our spirits have touched, and I say, Ho, it is good. The path grows strong with our walk. The field of the battle is all around. May it be a good battle. It is a good day to die. You, John, my brother, to my right, and you, Black Hawk, my brother, to my left. We stand as warriors, together. I pray that your children and mine may see spirit in all things. I pray that the human beings will walk together again as one spirit, as one race of people. My heart says this to you, John, there are many that walk the earth as warriors. Call to them, as my brother Black Hawk says, with the softness of the cloud-beings in your voice and the love of Mother Earth in your eyes, and they will come. Call to them and change will be once again. This is the way. I say to you, Hau Kola."

With tears in my eyes, I raised my hand. I hoped all the gratitude I felt for what Spotted Eagle had given me would come through these two words – "Hau Kola".

"My brother, Black Hawk," said Spotted Eagle. "My spirit soars to the heavens, as I have seen the eyes of my people as they once walked the earth. My eyes look to the path of the Grandfathers and Grandmothers, for it is bright again. I pray my journey is upon this path – the path of our people. I, Spotted Eagle, say to you with my heart full, Hau Kola."

"Hau Kola," said Black Hawk, raising his hand proudly.

"I will look to the stars for the time of the battle," Spotted Eagle said, "and will call to you, my brothers, and again we will stand as warriors, as the same spirit. Ho Tunkashila."

With those final words, in a flash of wind and feathers, I saw a beautiful eagle fly toward the heavens, a spotted eagle.

Chapter Twenty-Four

Black Hawk and I sat in silence for a long moment after Spotted Eagle had left us and flown higher and higher to the place of transition. I knew in my heart Black Hawk would also return soon. I watched him as he gazed across the farm with those black eyes seeing a feeling out there I knew to be the reflection of my soul. He sat as he had from the time I had met him – proud and rooted to the earth. What words were there to offer this warrior for all he had given me? The words and spirit that I hope are in these pages.

He had come to Woodstock, then had gone to South Dakota because that is where the path lay. He had said he could not turn his back. Perhaps he himself didn't know how he could have helped. But he knew if he walked the path of spirit with courage in his heart, the way would be shown. Hadn't it, I thought? Now, Spotted Eagle and I stood by his side. Spotted Eagle had said we stood as warriors together. For me there was no greater honor.

So perhaps here, by his example, was how I could make a difference. If I had faith and walked the path of spirit, of love, of rightness inside, the way would be clear to me.

Differences might be made without my knowing because from a breath of spirit we see only doing. The concern for outcomes is no more. Here was an example – Black Hawk.

Our eyes met. The bridge we had built stood strong.

Black Hawk smiled warmly and said, "John, we have come far from the place you sat for many seasons in Woodstock."

"Ho," I answered.

"To walk the path as a warrior is our way. It is what Tunkashila has given us. It is natural to us, as it is to the four-legged, and the winged, and the fish. Remember this, John, hold it in your heart. To act as warrior, to act with spirit is our way and the way of all human beings. Sometimes we get 'lost in the woods,' but our heart will find the way out if we open and ask. To see what is in front of you on the path, you must open your eyes!"

"Ho." I laughed along with him.

"Many will ask, where does the spirit come from? It comes from giving of yourself, from giving something back, from following the path of spirit. You show it honor in this way. A circle, John, do you see?" he asked, and outlined a circle with two fingers, as Spotted Eagle had.

I swept my two fingers away from my eyes.

"Remember, John, when you cross a stream, do you stop or keep walking up the path?"

"Keep walking."

"Ho, let what you have seen rest in the earth like a garden, and our Mother will give those seeds nourishment. The roots will grow deep, grow strong. They will stand tall and reach to Tunkashila."

"Do not hold what I have seen," I said. "Let it rest quiet

inside of me, so that its roots may grow deep. There is more to see. There is more knowing to see."

Black Hawk clasped his fingers together. "It is so, this is the path."

"With each breath, I walk a new path, the same but different. Paths of spirit," I said.

"You are not alone on your journey," Black Hawk said.

"We are all of the same spirit, all of the same hands," I answered back.

"Ho," Black Hawk confirmed.

The wind began to blow. The time was close. He stood, and I followed.

"My brother, you have, like the great bear, come from the winter sleep. You must see this time from the gathering many seasons ago as this. It is a time not lost, for each season has its place, its purpose. The great bear, our relative, wakes with the flowers as they begin to cover our Mother Earth. He wakes as the winged ones cross Grandfather Sky on their journey from the south. The season is new life. Here you will find the way."

"The great bear honors me with his gift of reflection," I stated.

The wind, my friend, suddenly grew stronger.

"John, time is not past, time is not future, it is with us forever. We see the innocence of our acts through this place. Acts of spirit have no time, remember this, my brother."

"Ho." My eyes burned with conviction and allegiance.

The sun, a orange ball of fire, began to come over the horizon. We looked together, and its light broke across us as we stood side by side on the earth of the farm. Side by side, as we had so often in these last days. The support of silence, silent reflection of one another. It was the path of no words.

We faced each other.

"My brother, one spark can carry the light of Tunkashila, a spark born in the heart," said Black Hawk.

"One spark," I said in whisper across to him.

"I, Black Hawk Who Walks the Wind, of the Sioux Nation, say to you, my brother, we walk the path of the warrior as one. You have honored me. May our children and their children and the children of the future walk the path of spirit. Hear me, my brother, I am in the rush of the stream, in the whiteness of the clouds, and in the many leaves of the Grandfather Trees. Here is where you will find me. Call to me, and we will once again walk the wind together, for our meeting is spoken on the rains which tell of newness. When it is the time of that meeting, it will once again be spoken on the softness of a breeze. We will stand as warriors again. My vision spoke of this. It is the path of spirit. It will be a good day to die."

"My heart will listen for your voice on the wind, my brother," I said. "I will stand with honor, as one with you. The battle will be great. It will be a good day to die."

We reached across the space separating us and clasped our forearms. We stood on the bridge together in a place of no time and no words.

The wind blew fierce over us, the pride we felt for each other in every gust. We stepped back and, with our heads high, raised our hands and spread our fingers wide; our eyes never left one another. We brought our hands against our chests and exchanged the final remembering, the final acknowledgment of the spirit in all.

"A Ho," I said to my friend, Black Hawk.

With a world resting behind each word, he responded, "A Ho." The wind exploded, and a black hawk flew to the clouds. My eyes followed him as he floated slowly on wings spread wide to the sun.

I stood alone, for the first time with my new eyes. I peered at the world around me. It was a beautiful world. A world for all races. Could I see change was possible from here? Yes, for I saw change was possible in me.

The path loomed in front of me.

I would return to Woodstock to collect my things, and say farewell to a town I must thank, for it had brought many lessons throughout the years.

From there, I don't know. But I must keep my heart open and have faith that the path of spirit will reveal itself. It is only there I can walk with a feeling of rightness and love inside. I must have faith.

We have come far, my friends. I hope the spirit in this book has touched your heart. The path for all races rises in front of us. I reach my hand out to you. May we walk with our heads high and with softness in our steps. May we come to the circle together as one – one spark that can start a great fire!

My friends, you have honored me by letting me share this book with you. I say to you, "A Ho."

The End

Quick Order Form

Order online at: www.SacredBear.com
or call toll-free: (877) 645-BEAR (2327)
Please have this information ready when placing an order:

Name: ______________________ Tel: ________________

Address: ______________________________________

City: ______________________ State: ____ Zip: ________

Email address: _________________________________

ITEM	PRICE	QTY	SUB. T
Between Eagle & Hawk print	$60.00		
The Woodstock Bridge book	$14.95		
Sales Tax if in Colorado: 8.5%			
Shipping By Air: **U.S.**: For print: $10.00, Book: $ 3.50 for first book & $1.00 for each additional book **International**: For Print: $35.00, Book: $7.00 for first book & $5.00 for each additional book	Shipping & Handling		
	TOTAL		$

Payment methods:

☐ Cheque ☐ Visa ☐ Mastercard ☐ Amex ☐ Discover

Card number: _________________________________

Name on card: _______________________ Exp. date: _____

www.WoodstockBridge.com

- Gregory Drambour's Recommended Reading List
- Speaking Engagements
- Book Signing Appearances
- Resource Guide
- Ebook version of *The Woodstock Bridge*
- Email the author